Skidboot

To Kate,
with best
regards

Ce[signature]

2014

Skidboot

The Smartest

DOG

In The World

A True Story written by Cathy Luchetti

Based on the Screenplay by Joel Carpenter & Guillermo Machado

Naretev Publishing
2113 Wells Branch Pkwy
Suite 6700
Austin, Texas 78728

Cover artwork © by Naretev Publishing

Cover design by Vlad Berea
Skidboot Photos Courtesy of Bob Ritchie and The Hartwig Family.

Publisher's Note: This story is based on Actual Events and although it is a work of nonfiction, some of the names, characters, places, and incidents have been fictionalized for privacy reasons. Locales and public names are sometimes used for atmospheric purposes. Any resemblance to actual people, living or dead, or to businesses, companies, events, institutions, or locales is completely coincidental.

Ordering Information:
Skidboot may be purchased for educational, business or promotional use. Special discounts are available on quantity purchases by corporations, associations, and others.

For more information contact the "Skidboot Sales Department" at the address above or by emailing Team Skidboot at **projectskidboot@gmail.com** or by visiting our website **www.project-skidboot.com**.

CONTENTS

CONTENTS

CONTENTS

In memory of my brother, Francis Colligan, who called me up a few years ago and said, "Cathy, have you ever heard of a dog called Skidboot?"

Author's Note: The warp and woof of Skidboot's life is true to fact…but with a tweak or two. Chronology gives way to story, with the belief that a good narrative often creates its own detours. Many situations are conceived as possibilities within the story's context. Names are altered for the sake of privacy. Some good citizens of Quinlan, Texas might be fuddled by these changes, but consider this creative nonfiction, Texas style.

"I had long been of the opinion that dogs are much cleverer than men. I also believed that they could talk, and that only a certain obstinacy kept them from doing so."

— Nikolai Gogol, "Memoirs of a Madman"

"God gives you a dog, you do the responsible thing. He gives you an extra smart dog, you go where that leads you."

— David Hartwig

FOREWORD

by

Dr. Steven "Bo" Keeley, Worldwide Veterinarian,
Commodities Consultant, World champion racquetball star,
and author of
'Executive Hobo, Riding the American Dream'

I grew up sneaking kibble from dog dishes before becoming a veterinarian and consider my taste in canine books highly trained. This book is gourmet. A blend, not a mix because that wouldn't be authentic. This book recalls John McCormick's *Fields and Pastures*, James Herriot's *All Creatures Great and Small*, and certainly Louis L'Amour's great story telling, along with a dash of scientific spice. *Skidboot* is the smartest dog in the world, a fictionalized biography that will have you scratching the kennels for pups that might grow up or be like the protagonist, and searching the bookshelves for more Cathy Luchetti animal stories and true westerns. Skidboot the real dog and *Skidboot,* the biography based on the screenplay, are destined to follow Lassie and Rin Tin Tin straight past Snoopy into the hearts of every reader and become the next mischievous, loveable and, yes, most intelligent, advisor to humankind.

ACKNOWLEDGEMENTS

Special thanks to David Hartwig for freely sharing his story, for his candid reminiscences as well as many colorful, probing, psychological insights. To Joel and Guillermo, whose lively screenplay provided the roadmap, and to my son Zachary Luchetti, for editing advice and his ever-creative phrasing. Thanks to my husband, Peter Hadreas, for his loving support and excellent advice. And to Rebecca and Myles Colligan, niece and nephew. And to Veterinarian Steve Keeley, for his doggone helpful insights.

PROLOGUE

"Skidboot?" Oprah flashed her huge smile. The dog put out his paw. Oprah looked terrific in lavender while Skidboot's green kerchief wasn't bad. Dressing a dog for national television made David Hartwig uneasy, but so did everything else on this Tuesday morning on the Oprah show. Here he was anyway, nerves or not, and so was his dog. *Better just get through it.*

Reporters called his dog "Zen like," which might or might not be true. Skidboot had lockfire concentration and right now, he was frozen into pointer position, one paw curled up, nose straight, staring at the toy.

"What's he doing, David?" Oprah beamed another of her crowd-pleasing smiles.

"He's sneaking up on his toy." David choked back the word "ma'am" and smiled instead. "It may sound simple but he's got his own style." On command, Skidboot advanced in panther mode, belly low, stalking, eyes fixed, barely moving, not a muscle out of place. Inch by inch, he drew closer.

"Now stop."

The dog froze, eyes pinpoints.

By now everyone who tuned in knew that Skidboot was waiting for the count of three to magically break free and claim his toy.

"One – two – six – seven –fourteen – twenty nine."

You could feel the frustration.

"...seventeen – forty – five- twelve..."

There were about 9 million more numeric combinations he could cite, but Hartwig could feel the crowd's anxiety as they watched the dog, frozen as a popsicle. They were anxious because they wanted the dog to do well, to not move, and to not screw up. They didn't trust that an animal could obey for this length of time. Hartwig looked bored with it all until softly, like an oversight, he slipped in "three."

Skidboot collapsed onto the toy. Oprah drew in her breath and clapped while five hundred people roared. David Hartwig stood there, stunned again, for the hundredth time, that he was on live television leading his Blue Heeler through his paces. Just a few weeks ago in a taxi heading down Fifth Avenue in New York, he told the cabbie that he was a simple man who lived in a double wide on a small ranch in a pit stop in Texas and had no idea what he was doing here. The cab driver nodded sympathetically but wasn't convinced. They were headed for NBC after all. Really?

The question that the cabbie didn't ask was bound to come up.

Oprah was the next one to ask it.

"David, how did you and Skidboot get started with all this?"

Slowly, as if on cue, Skidboot turned around and stared at David, almost as if Oprah had asked him the question. He stared long and hard, as if searching the man's face for an answer, and finding something familiar there, something that felt like what he wanted, Skidboot relaxed. And in that moment when the tension flowed out, everyone swears that the dog smiled.

David Hartwig was used to this and so was Skidboot. They looked at each other. It had been one heck of journey, and longer than a hound's tooth.

CHAPTER ONE

Heeler History

The Blue Heeler dropped her litter behind a granite outcropping in the Australian outback. She was agile, muscular, rank as a wolf. She turned and tongue-slapped her puppies into the world, grooming them with every lick, calming the tiny hearts that raced with excitement. The world made them squirm--Grass! Sky! Wind!--but her tongue relaxed them, helped them secrete more digestive juices to better absorb food, while their bodies rocked in a healing sea of neurochemicals. These chemicals are not much different than those the pharmaceutical world buys and sells: beta-endorphins, oxytocins and more. Soon she pushed them aside and stood up, shaking her pelt. Her tail hung at a slight curve. Her feet were round with short toes. Her skull was broad with wide-set ears, but her coat marked her as a Heeler, generally known as an Australian cattle dog. She wore a smooth, dense coat of frosty grey and black, oddly speckled with blue. She glanced down at the pups and almost sneered. Poor things. They were solid white. It would be months before their beautiful speckled coats grew in.

She shook herself. Time to get back to work. Every Australian cattle dog worked hard and loved to work. She had taken enough vacation from her job of herding cattle. Heelers could nip and snap a herd into shape faster than any man on a horse. Proudly, they worked the stock, fast and forceful, able to drive the cattle for days under a sweltering sun, through blinding desert sandstorms.

The Australian pioneers of the 1800's were creative survivors, beefing up the weak English breeds of dog that could never handle the rigors of the new continent. One veterinarian in Sydney threw Dingo, Kelpie, German Shepherd, and Kangaroo Hound into the mix, creating a breed swift as a snake, and tough. This odd lot mongrel made its way to the United States and was known as the Australian Cattle Dog of America, aka, the Blue Heeler. This new dog probably had traces of Dingo plus Blue Merle Collie, possibly Dalmatian and even Bull Terrier

There in the outback three of her puppies lived and mated, and it was good. Their puppies lived and it was also good. As each succeeding generation sprang forth, they proved more able, agile and cooperative than the former, and it became ever better. The breed allowed marginal dirt farmers to profit at round-up time because one dog equaled at least two men, and the dogs cost a lot less. The Australian Cattle dog stands as the unofficial mascot for the Australian beef industry. And on it went, a canine genealogy that finally found its way to Texas, where a pup was born that nearly bridged the symbiotic animal-to-human gap, with the potential to become a canine soul mate as well as a work engine, a furry phenomenon.

This dog showed supersensory powers that outstripped ordinary dogs, who only possess the ability to detect cancers, announce earthquakes, and howl at barometric pressure changes. Avid as a three-year-old, this dog could understand a glance, a word, a gesture, and act accordingly.

This dog would be the canine manifestation of Einstein's theory of a unified field, where everything, even species, interact with eerie prescience and are part of life's great interconnectedness. A dog born to bond, he needed someone empathic, a lover of animals, who could tune himself to "listen" as well as to instruct. Someone who lived as a cowboy rancher on a plot of land in Quinlan, Texas--David Hartwig.

CHAPTER TWO

Rodeo Life

A hot Texas sun blazed over the arena, and already the rodeo fans were guzzling beer, trying to cool off. The Mesquite, Texas rodeo arena was no different than a hundred others, a semicircle of wooden benches facing a gladiatorial ring where men battled beasts and each other, winner take all.

David Hartwig was striving to be that winner. He felt the win inside him, like a fist. He'd always had this special knowledge about himself when it came to two things: sports and animals. You might say, he possessed animal spirits, an energy that pushed him through championship swimming right into the roping arena.

Nerves jumping, he fingered the rope like a rosary, seeking help, wanting that prize. *Sometimes I pray myself from one side to the other,* he thought, knowing that energy and faith could propel him right through this boot heel existence, straight into a national roping championship. Today he was riding in the Mesquite, Texas Pro Rodeo outside of Dallas, a homespun little operation that would someday draw crowds and celebrities, but was now, still, just a local show. He'd turned down a swimming scholarship to Southern Methodist University to be here, or at least, to be a world champion.

I'm still in the holding pen, he thought. No championship, no scholarship. Just that pervasive inner voice that assured him, *it's ok.* And he knew it *was* ok. A hard-headed man, he never backed down. Even as a skinny kid who looked like a walking bully magnet, if anyone even touched him, they'd end up on the ground so fast that not even David knew what happened. *I was never a fighter,* he thought. Not consciously. All he knew was that he never backed down.

He turned to locate Barbara in the crowd, then remembered their little argument. Nothing serious, but she'd huffed off and he knew he'd ride without her support today. They both believed that she brought him luck, and if she was in the stands, then all would go well. Well, he'd ride without her then, so much for lucky charms.

Eyes narrowed, he watched the calf bolt into the arena. Another flash brought in Randy Coyle, resident champion calf roper and personal nemesis, a cocky 30-year-old whose relatives ran the rodeo. Nepotism never hurt a man's chances of raking in prizes, David thought. No sir.

Stomach churning, David watched Coyle sail his rope neatly over the calf, shoot off the saddle and slam himself into it, upending the calf so fast it forgot to bawl. With three loops of piggin' string, Coyle bound up the calf's legs, stiff as firewood. Then he flung himself away, strutted toward his horse, and swung himself easily into the saddle with the same jaunty insolence he'd shown ten minutes earlier. He'd seen David in the john, hurling over the cracked toilet.

"Sick again, Hartwig?" He'd winked, laughed, and slammed the door shut on a man's private anxiety. David tried to get over the embarrassment. He couldn't understand himself: if he knew he could win, why get so nervous? Calves, dusty and tag-eared, shuffled through the chute toward the spring-loaded doors. One squeezed in and the door slammed behind it. His calf.

"Welcome David Hartwig!" The announcer lobbed his microphone around like a magic wand, predicting a *special feelin'* about *this up'n'comer from Quinlan Texas!* David felt the same way.

Settling down, he turned stone cold. Determined. *That's the stuff, what he'd been waiting for.*

He nodded for the calf. Minutes exploded into seconds. The gate banged open, the calf shot out, and David felt Hank lunge under him. The rope sailed overhead, looping the calf's neck as Hank braked to a shuddering halt, his skid boots trailing dust. Skid boots are a protective sleeve around the horse's heel, reinforcing Hank's heels and shanks as his skidding hooves dragged through the hard-packed caliche soil of the rodeo arena. The calf sailed through the air, landing with a thud.

David flung himself off, sprinted to the brawling animal and flipped it upend. Gnawing at the piggin' string between his teeth, he clutched its legs, feeling the weight of a fifty-pound calf pull against him as he roped the legs together, shouting *two wraps and a hooey!* Hank held the rope taut, moving steadily backwards. David signaled "time." He strained to hear the count.

"One one thousand, two one thousand…we got a tie!"

Roars, music, confusion. Tension gripped them. Yells of support, bets placed, animosity rampant. Hank, trained to release the calf rather than drag it pitifully around the way some did, slackened the rope. David glared at Randy. Randy glared back. David scanned the bleachers to see Barbara. Instead, he caught Russell's eye and waved as the eleven-year-old jumped up and waved his hat, shouting, "Way to go, you got it!"

What a good kid. His stepson, his fan. He needed the support, and he knew the deck was stacked. The loudspeaker blared like a tornado warning, "the judges have spoken, the 1991 Mesquite calf-roping winner is Randy Coyle!" Naw, David thought, the uncle has spoken. It was pure hooey, Texas style.

As if mind-reading, Coyle thrust at him, chin out. "You got a problem, boy?

David's anger surged. All those years, now come to this. Effort and opportunities given away like coupons, so that somebody's uncle could tilt the deck. He spat on the ground, fists tight at his sides. Then he saw Barbara in the stands. *She'd come, after all.*

"You cheat!" Russell had run down from the stands and blurted out, looking surprised as he did it.

"Hey, that boy of yours at least is man enough to speak up. Maybe he should do the ropin," Coyle guffawed, his barely sprouted moustache jiggling. He flirted up from under his wide hat, looking for others to join in.

David moved toward him, then felt Barbara grab his arm. He knew it wasn't worth it. Jealousy was the trademark of a small mind — so said Mark Twain--and he was not small-minded. Coyle was a bitterness to him, but he'd get over it.

"Maybe you better give it up, Hartwig. It'd be better on your con-sti-tution!" Coyle bent over, laughing, while Russell flushed, stared at David, then back at the cowboy. David grabbed his stepson and they hustled after Barbara, back to the safety of his 30-acres in Quinlan, Texas.

CHAPTER THREE

Quinlan, Texas

If a Dingo-bred dog chose a new home outside ancestral Australia, it would be Texas. If unlucky, it would end up West Texas, needled by cactus, dodging rattlers, pining for a better terrain, even though the hills rolled gently, and Spring brought a carpet of green and more bluebirds than a Disney film. North Texas, Hunt County, close to Quinlan, suffered great heat yet also the relief of rain, given the right time of year. Such rain kept the Sabine river rushing toward its historic outflow in Mexico, bringing with it flowing memories, history, and tales of a Caddoan tribe, the Tawakoni, that sheltered near its banks, fought the Comanche, Apache, and the Osage, and later "molested" any nearby Spanish, as well as later unfortunate U.S. settlers. Finally forced onto a reservation in 1837, all that remains of the tribe today is Tawakoni Lake, the word meaning "River Bend Among Red Sand Hills," but which might also mean, "river built by backhoe and cement mixer." The town of Quinlan naps close by, its lakeside condos offering worry-free lakefront living just a shout away from Burgers & Fries, a popular dining spot. A nearby oil pipeline continues to uphold a clean safety record, a record in itself.

First settled in the 16th century by the Spanish, generations of farmers, ranchers, and buckaroos rolled through the area, followed generations later by David Hartwig, who craved open space as far away from Dallas as he could find. Groomed suburbs depressed him. Cosmopolitan life bored him. In his mind lay the cowboy idyll of free range, wild horses, rodeos, dogs, and adventure. His father, Rudy Hartwig, taught high school math and science, his mother Pat worked as a secretary, and the family lived an orderly if noisy life of four sons and countless dogs, which his father kept in steady supply from the local pound.

Long and lanky, David swam the freestyle as State Champion for two years running, even if he didn't particularly like swimming. But faced with *any* sport, the same kick-start determination he'd had at the rodeo would overwhelm him, dark and aggressive, ready to spring out and *win*. Despite a gawky frame, poor choices, and feeling trapped as a house pet, he knew things about himself that made him both restless and oddly confident. So confident that he turned down college, choosing a profession straight out of the middle ages, a farrier.

"A what?" Some friends were astonished, others, mostly his long-time friends, knew why horseshoeing prevailed over a full swimming scholarship from SMU. A true maverick, David had turned down this bastion of Texas excellence to follow the rodeo, shoe horses, and win the state championship calf roping title. His parents got it, even if they didn't agree.

They'd seen his excitement in the 11th grade, in that Vocational Ag class, when he managed to get a job on a 60-acre ranch and then broke his first horse. How? He'd just had this *feeling* that when he walked his 200-lb. calf around the field, which he had to do to keep it healthy, that if he walked the unbroken mare along with the calf and kept it to the calf's left, they'd socialize. And slowly, the cow would *teach* the mare how to be a roping horse.

"It's stupid. Why walk the calf around every day by itself when you could be getting them used to each other?" His father could only agree, wondering if the boy could figure out a way to go commercial with such insights.

CHAPTER FOUR

The Christmas Puppy

Christmas was not going well. Like some twisted Dickens plot, Barbara teetered on losing her job, David was broke, Quinlan Power and Gas had docked their electricity and he was flat out of gas money. He sighed. About the only stable thing these days was his stepson, who seemed more starry-eyed about David with every passing failure, a weird father complex syndrome that he'd never seen in animals because, well, animals had more sense. Russell did *not* lack brains, in fact he was an excellent student, until he somehow crossed neural paths with David and emerged as a half cowboy, all honor student. The half cowboy part irked Barbara, whose glance seemed to say *one cowpoke in the family is enough.*

David accepted his role in this. If he put away the rodeo dream, maybe they'd have more than a scrawny Christmas tree, cheap presents, and that bucket in the middle of the floor full of rain water. Even their rusting doublewide felt broken, and mountain of bills on the kitchen counter grew like mold. Their electricity blinked on and off like a crazy thing. They struggled, with no way to catch up.

He felt like a country western version of himself, a cowboy so *downtrodden, so busted and oh so ashamed.* He wondered if feeling special really meant *specially broke.*

And Russell, well. The boy wore his hat high and his jeans low, and school kids teased him about his rodeo dad. If he bragged about David, they jeered at him, which drove him to a fury. David's occasional roping shortfalls were turning out to be his stepson's burden.

The phone rang, a good sign, because it meant it was still paid for. The shrill jangle bounced off the metal walls, sharp as an axe. Butch Jones' voice gruffed over the line, and yes, David could come right away to shoe his horse. He'd run into Butch one night, an embarrassing deal at the EZ Mart gas station, when he and Russell had found themselves out of gas, with a check in hand but post dated until after Christmas. Russell loved to cheer his David up, and made a game out of finding' spare coins to "help" with the budget, deep-diving in the dusty truck for orphan nickels, random dimes, hopeful pennies. *Look,* he'd yell, bringing up a sticky quarter pried from the floor mat. Or *here we go* as he tried to unstick two dimes from the wad of gum. *Still wasn't enough for gas,* David realized. Russell tried to distract him.

"You ever hear why the little strawberry was so upset?

"No."

"She was in a jam!" David grinned at the familiar punch line. They both laughed.

The handful of sticky coins might just get them home. The youngster tending counter sniggered at Russell's flushed face. Both boys went to school together, and David could already hear the taunts his boy would have to suffer. Suddenly, a hand slapped down a $20 bill on the counter. "Take this, boys," and David recognized the gruff voice of his neighbor, Butch Jones.

"No *sir!*" David moved to shove the money back, but Butch moved to quiet him.

"Son, I got a family situation coming up and I need your help." With fresh snow and eager kids, he'd promised the family a sleigh ride, only the horses were unshod for the event. Since David was coming over anyway, what harm to advance him some on the horseshoeing work, what say?

"I appreciate the offer, Butch." David straightened up, no longer a poor penitent but a man with a mission. When it snowed in Quinlan, it meant that David made money. For an unshod horse, snow could be a nightmare. While the rest of town cozily watched icy white feathers drift over the hills, blurring the sun at the edges, and causing the geese to flap in frustration at being trapped in Texas, it meant money for him. For unshod horses, show could be a nightmare. An unshod horse with a naturally balanced hoof, a dense hoof horn and a sole with a rim had traction and could pull itself through freezing ice. But flat hooves might bruise on the frozen ground. Or, a horse might have a natural indent that trapped the ice and caused the animal to "snowball" or skid.

David would examine the hoof with the sharp gaze of an orthopod, then diagnose the best traction option, straight out of the *Hoof Care Manual*. He might use aluminum shoes or a surfacing material such as tungsten carbide, or maybe Borium, smeared over the horse's regular metal shoe. Or nails. If he used two nails per shoe, his total bill, with time, might be close to $125.00. That should tide them over until the other check went through.

The truck sputtered, nearly empty again, but at least the headlights worked. White shimmers of light wove through the snow veils, an exotic dance of light and shadow. Snow carpeted the penned horse, its head sunk low.

Not in the barn? David bent himself to the icy maelstrom, trying to sooth the horse to make the work safe. He had to crouch in the cold with a hoof the size of a toaster in his lap. A nervous horse could kick you to Saturday, and the last thing he needed was an injury.

"Russell, keep the lights on!" he shivered, nearly dropping the hoof. He figured that two nails would do it and began to tap them in. But Russell had jumped out of the truck and run to the barn. Minutes later he shouted, *come look, David, over here!*

David pushed away from the horse and creaked to his feet. Although in his thirties, he still felt agile as a teenager, except when popsicled in the snow for an hour. He straightened up, hobbling toward the barn where a stray bitch, recently crawled into the hayloft from who-knows-where, nursed a brood of Blue Heeler puppies. *If I wanted a dog I'd get a Blue Heeler,* David thought idly, as the Heeler was the ideal round-up and work dog in Texas.

Only he didn't want a dog, he only wanted to finish up and head back to the trailer, where he might be able to snuggle up to his wife and keep warm.

His wife! Realization slammed through him--he didn't have a Christmas present for Barbara. The puppies writhed around, tumbling, chirruping, sucking, mewling. Cute enough. Why, he'd get her one! It shamed him that Barbara had to work so hard, ten years now as a legal aid at the municipal courthouse, her knowledge and skill far above her pay scale. Whenever she flashed this ability, her supervisor, Earle, got testy. Earle watched her, hawk eyes narrowed, fat cheeks shiny with anticipation. He waited for her to screw up, and a single minute tardy was his time to pounce.

"Late again, Barbara."

"You only got this job because your daddy was a military man, and we respect that around here."

"We can always make other arrangements here, you know."

Her workplace bristled with opposition, like an enemy military zone with guns trained, triggered, and ready to fire. When she quietly tried to counsel people, Earle would pop up and reprimand her. It irked him that she knew so much law and he wanted to make sure no one went away with her free non-lawyer opinions.

No wonder she acted cold, no longer the clinging girl he'd met at 27, who took one look at his shirtless, sun-buttered length and came straight over, asked his name, and never again left his side. He'd been helping her with her first horse, a half-broken 2-yr. old, the culmination of her childhood dreams. As a girl in California, she'd loved horses. But now, in addition to the horse, she fell in love with him.

A colorful courtship, he'd often said, filled with breakups, reunions more breakups, and then more reunions. David had been admired by his share of women, some who tried to get his attention by offering to help him bale hay. They'd sweep the mixed-grass hay up into windrows, the simplest job ever, expecting praise and flirtation but finding instead an extreme perfectionism that brought scowls and epitaphs at their sloppiness, or at how they threw their rakes on the ground for someone to step on. He'd harass them about their hay piles, treating them like hired help while they pouted, sweeping back their hair.

Barbara had gotten herself a headstrong man, a demanding perfectionist who yelled, cussed, ordered people around and insisted *no short cuts* and *push the limits*. Ask his parents, Pat and Rudy, and they'd remember the temper tantrums he threw, lying on the floor like he was dying, stubborn and unrelenting until he got his way. Thus life flew along — exciting, uncomfortable and fast paced. And when marriage finally jammed them together, they understood both sides of *better or worse*.

"Russell, pick one out. We'll see if it's ok with Butch to give it to Barbara."

Russell stared at the puppies, and locked in on a fat, variegated one with bright eyes and a bulging tummy, signs of a lively alpha. The pup stretched out his sleek head and licked David's hand.

"Yep, that's the one." Butch approved, wishing they'd take a couple more home. A pup in the hand meant one less to feed, but they said no and bundled up the chosen one, yapping and whimpering. David pulled up tall and stood looking down at the mother, content amid the suckling, smacking and yipping. The fat pup already strained to get back, and they gripped it more tightly. In the corner, David noticed another dog, thinner, more fierce, lurking back in the shadows, staring at them, eyebrows cocked, its eyes brimming with what, amusement? Or curiosity, he couldn't place it.

CHAPTER FIVE

The Exchange

Five minutes later, David slammed on the brakes. The truck skidded sideways and Russell looked at him, inquiring. David suddenly knew what had been bothering him. That other puppy, the smaller one, had given him a *look*. It was a challenge, the same kind Randy Coyle threw down, the same kind he felt when the gun went off and he flew into the middle lane, swimming. That puppy had communicated, while the other one — and he glanced down, seeing the fat ball of fur playing with its own paws — was just having fun.

"Russell, we got to revisit this puppy choice."

Russell looked surprised. The fat puppy stopped fiddling for a moment and also looked surprised.

"That other dog, son, he had *something*. We need to go back and find out what."

Minutes later, they slipped Fat Boy back into the brood and stepped back to watch. The big pup eagerly clamped itself onto the mother's teat, sucking, drooling, and wagging its tail. Cute as anything, and certainly more cute than the other pup poised at the rear, alert as an owl, head cocked, guarding the nest. That pup caught his gaze and held it. Then it seemed to relax, his muscles sagging briefly under his thin coat. *They came back.*

"Russell?" David queried.

"You betcha," Russell scooped up the puppy, which first resisted, rigid and fierce, its nails splayed. But sheltered in the boy's arms, the dog relaxed again. David pried open the dented truck door and prayed for start-up. It was time to head home. As the truck chugged on fumes, they stared at the new Hartwig. What would they name him?

Famous show dogs paraded through their thoughts. Lassie, the show dog. Rin Tin Tin, who sprang from a litter of bombed-out puppies found in a kennel in the German Lorraine, named after French children's finger puppets that they gave to the American soldiers for good luck. There was a litany of "Wonder Dogs," starting with Ace the wonder dog, a German Shepherd in the 1930's, as famed a star as Lassie in his day. Then came Pal the Wonder Dog, Rex the Wonder Dog, and all the Wonder Dogs to follow. "Wonder Dog" was out, but David and Russell both agreed that if left to Barbara, they'd end up with Spot, or Pumpkin, or worse. Names burst out: "Bob Wire," "Hot Shot," "T-Post," "Lasso." They laughed together, their disjointed cowboy rap shooting back and forth.

"Let's hold off, then." David concentrated on the road ahead, puzzling through mounds of braided snow and ice slicks toward the spot of light beaming through the curtains, a warm homecoming.

Blizzards roared so occasionally in North Texas that each was a rarity. For kids, snow meant closed schools and popcorn days, but David would rather have blue pigs than falling snow. The lights were off, the heat was off, and they were in for a session of maximum mobile home discomfort. He was sure he'd paid the bill. But maybe it was the lag time that now put them in the dark. Lag time always got you.

Barbara flashed the battery light, its beam like a warm pool of welcome.

"Russell, this is the right dog. Let's not bungle it with the wrong name." They nodded, grinned, but failed to see the dog grin back.

CHAPTER SIX

Barbara's Surprise

Barbara was not happy. She'd fallen out with her boss, Earl, again, a conflicted man who circled her like prey, ready to pounce for the tiniest error. She couldn't help herself, but when people came into the courthouse needing information, she gladly gave it. But what had it gotten her?

The trailer door shook as the men blew in, stamping ice, shivering, scraping boots and battling it closed against the wind. The trailer shuddered like an old Frigidaire. Barbara noticed right away that David seemed hurt, bent over himself in a weird way. She imagined a horse kick, him being laid up, no work...

"What happened?"

"Horse kicked me, shoulder out." David sidled into the trailer, nearly knocking over the floor lamp. In the dark, the EZ boy rocker lunged at him, and he tripped backwards. Ouch! The battery lamp swiveled his way, and, sure enough, Barbara saw he was hurt, heard him making a strange sound, like whimpering. He straightened up, opening his jacket to expose the damage but she saw only a tiny face, staring at her. What was it, a bat? It had pointed ears, a black face, and piercing eyes.

"Merry Christmas, hon." David swept his coat open and the puppy huffed at her, an explosion of sound. Nose first, it wriggled along David's arm to inspect her, as Barbara stared back, surprised. They held eye contact until the puppy let out an approving yip.

"Oh look at that!" In a second, the puppy was in her arms, squirming, nestling its butt into the crook of her elbow, licking her upside one arm and down the other. It knew instantly that this woman offered safe haven, much like a mother Heeler. Warm and nurturing, she would be his place of refuge, of food, of defense. For a dog just born, this one had already learned a lot. He sighed, *finally*.

Christmas found David, Russell and Barbara huddled together, a cluster of Hartwigs mulling over the newest addition to their home, the Heeler named...

"What...?" Barbara scrolled through the possibilities. They laughed at the Hollywood dogs, Axelrod the Basset Hound, Cheeka the Pug, Gidget the Chihuahua, Honey Tree Evil Eye, even Lassie, Buck, Cosmo, or Higgins. Then David and Russell added their cowboy litany, but she didn't hear anything she liked. It sounded like a rodeo roster.

"Let him play," she instructed, and the puppy slid to the floor, claws splayed for balance, wobbling off but soon gaining traction. Barbara thought, *warm milk*, and the puppy waddled after her toward the kitchen, throwing a triumphant glance back at David.

"Oh, he's following me!"

Then the dog veered off, attention caught by a woven straw basket in the corner. It pulled itself up over the edge of the basket and studied David's loose collection of old rodeo gear. This was the Basket of Failed Dreams, where the paraphernalia of calf roping gathered dust, where occasionally he'd dig through and sort out something useful, like one of his many pairs of skid boots, or leather shin protectors. A rodeo horse without skid boots was like, well, a ballerina without slippers, and he had a skid boot for every occasion. The basket reminded him of his early passion for the calf ropin' heroes, like Toots Mansfield, seven time world champion calf roper, who won more buckles, saddles, trophies, awards and honors than any other tie-down calf roper in history, a legend in the Frontier Times Museum's Texas Heroes Hall of Honor. Toots could levitate a calf with his huge hands and lay it down faster than any man alive. People sent their sons from all over the world to Mansfield's roping school on his ranch outside Big Springs, Texas, where Saudi, Scotch, Canadian and Australian teens teetered on the corral fence, stiff in new jeans and new boots to learn to sail a lariat loop through the air, easy as smoke. Maybe if he'd gone to *that* school instead of Dallas High, some of the speed and dexterity of the master would have rubbed off.

Regret had drained out of him long ago, leaving a thin film of worn out ambition. He still possessed some memorable events, though, like the time he'd scored 45 straight calves in a row for practice, some kind of record, since the usual practice was, tops, fifteen calves using two to three horses. Hearing his friend yell, "go plumb wild, kid!!" and he did.

"Bang! The basket upended, spurs clanked on the floor, and the puppy shuddered backwards, trying to free its paw from entanglement in a leather skid boot that smelled richly of horse fetlock. The pup yipped itself wild, huffing and gnawing, cart-wheeling around on the floor. It was odd behavior for something so small, and they watched it with curiosity. Leather frayed as the dog snarled and rocked, slapping the skid boot right, then left, as if killing prey.

David pulled the boot loose and sailed it across the floor. The puppy shot after it and worried it around. David retrieved the boot and flung it behind the television. Again, the dog shot after the boot, growling low in its chest, a primal sound.

"Skidboot!" Barbara brightened, "we'll call him Skidboot." David and Russell stared at the moving entanglement at their feet, a leather horse contraption atop four paws and a tail that thumped like a mutant centipede on the shag carpet, beating up dust into the air, pure comedy. They'd seen enough. Somehow it made sense to name this dog after a horse's support device, worn like gladiatorial armor to keep it from being hurt.

Like an omen, the lights flicked on, followed by the comforting hum of the refrigerator, and the radio's *Noel, Noel.* Light as air, a sense of serenity fell upon them. Barbara enfolded Russell, David enfolded Barbara, and they clustered, tight as burrs, to watch the antics of the newest member of the Hartwig family. Peace flowed like a river, and the rough edges they'd patched together seemed strong and workable. The puppy snuggled them, inhaling the scent of his new family. Later, they yawned, stretched, and headed for bed, leaving Skidboot in a cardboard box surrounded by treats — baby milk bones, a chocolate Santa, kibble. Special treats for Christmas.

So peaceful. And so unexpected when hours later, the tree tilted and crashed to the floor. Lights splintered, glass ornaments cracked. David thumped up in the dark, dizzy from sleep, tripping into a scene of such destruction that he thought he was dreaming: the tree rose up like a pine Titanic. A devilish face dangled ribbon from its gargoyle mouth, half hidden under the remains of the sofa cushions. Bleary, nearly staggering, David recoiled from a sensation so disgusting, so visceral, that he'd almost rather have stepped on a snake, at least then he could just blow its head off. Instead, he squished hopelessly into a pile of puppy poop to view the remains of the room. Dung welled up between his toes. He hopped barelegged toward the bathroom and threw himself into the tub, hearing Russell call out and Barbara answer. By then they were all awake, wide-eyed at the sticky tracks, the up-heaved papers, the shredded presents. Over there, the jacket they'd scrimped to buy Russell, the one with the cool zippers, lying in limp blue pieces. On the carpet, the remains of that pretty silk scarf Barbara liked so much. The tree tilted like a dying thing, its lights blinking "help."

"Skidboot!" They roared in unison, "Noooooo!! *Bad dog!*"

"Noooo, bad dog!" turned into the dog's real name. *No, bad dog!* harassed the baby calves, running them silly. *No, bad dog!* redesigned socks, ate underwear, and scent-marked everyone's clothing, finishing each piece by flipping it into the air to catch on fixtures on the way down. *No, bad dog!* polished off lunch by snacking on a shoe, usually one of Barbara's. *No, bad dog!* peed on David's LazyBoy rocker, the puddle so deep that it shorted out the television and cost them a week's work to get it back and running. David, angry, once hoisted the puppy overhead, but Barbara intervened.

"Poor baby," she'd say, holding out her arms, unaware of Skidboot's raised eyebrow, cocked at David. Oddly, the puppy reminded him of his childhood, of being teased by neighborhood kids. Although Skid's dark eyes, unblinking, held something other than mockery, something he'd never seen in a dog before, a kind of intelligence that caused the dog to tremble with...something. Maybe the need to communicate, to tell him...something. What was it, a challenge? An offer of friendship? An insult?

Meanwhile, shredded newspaper fluttered around the trailer, mingled with fugitive feathers, mounds of poop and gnawed toys. They might wonder *whose feathers*, and also *why so destructive*? Skidboot was a home wrecker whom his wife, for unexplained reasons, protected unduly. If he banished Skidboot to the barn, Barbara cradled the mutt, nuzzled it, and said to David, "*You* go sleep in the barn!" She was joking, of course, but jokes score only if there's truth behind them. At times, David wondered, who's in charge? The dog? Truth be told, the situation was getting out of hand.

CHAPTER SEVEN

Bad Dog

The possibility of a throwback to the wild Australian dingo had crossed his mind. Dingo packs wiped out the entire population of Tasmanian devils as well as a prevalent population of Black-tailed Native hens. Dingoes ravaged sheep herds from one side of the continent and down the other. Even though the puppy was an American, he was also a mutt hybrid who could throw himself into compulsive fits so primal, so self-defeating, and so congested that it seemed almost demonic, or more kindly stated, OCD, or "Out Of Control Dog." The only difference between this pup and its wild forbearers was that dingoes had short periods of rest between dawn and dusk.

What's wrong with you? David thought as he watched the dog windmill around their tight trailer, mouth snapping, saliva flying, shaking himself into a frenzy. A grocery bag, Barbara's shoe, an unsecured personal item threw it into a hyper-drive of yipping, panting, shaking, gnawing, followed by prey-dragging the item off into a recondite corner beneath the trailer where the panting, heaving and growling mounted with embarrassing intensity. The sight of a stuffed toy turned him insane. He moaned, howled, kicked his legs into a frenzy and gnashed his sharp teeth. Skidboot could repurpose a tennis ball into shreds in a minute flat. He could dismember a doll as quick as eating cobbed corn. And the more he ripped things apart, the more obsessed he became. Skidboot knew no limits, and the family sank beneath a tsunami of destruction that roared through their daily lives. In more forgiving moments, David thought *ambition,* followed by another thought, *mayhem,* followed by some punishment or another, usually insignificant.

"Into the barn!" David roared.

"This is not your dog to throw around," Barbara read his mind and scooped Skidboot up, nuzzling him, and David *saw the puppy smile!* But even without Barbara the dog held his ground. A handsome animal by now, rounds and hollows once thin had filled out, his sleek flanks glowing with mottled flecks of blue. If such confused coloring turned up on a flower, it would be a toxic bloom warning its predators away. His coat was mottled, as if someone had shaken oil with blue and white paint, then jiggled it around so that it flecked and spotted but never really mixed. Skidboot often lay, snout in paws, watching David with such intensity that David's back hairs crawled. It was like being stalked by a resting cougar. He felt as if Skidboot were relaying a message, broadcasting from inner space in a different language — *in doggerel*--urgently as possible. *Let's get to it,* the dog conveyed. *Now.*

They headed toward the truck, ready to go to town. David had a few invoices to drop off and hopefully one to collect. It may seem petty, but replacing the dog's damage was getting expensive. He looked out over the wide expanse of Texas, which was still home to a festival of creeping, flying, slithering and stalking mammals and reptiles that prevailed in spite of the onset of malls, parking lots, highways, back roads and power installations. Mockingbirds poked fun from telephone poles, and scissor-tailed flycatchers sheared through the air. Rattlers curled invisible in the dust, awaiting some misstep. Bats and rats frolicked. Foxes lurked in the scrub forests and tall grasses of the north hill country and coyotes howled down the stars at night.

He swerved the old Ford to avoid the Texas state mammal, a nine-banded armadillo slugging its way across State Route 34, a probable victim of one of the big farm pick-ups barreling back and forth. One of the earliest border-crossers, this strange mammal made its way from Mexico by self-inflating, sucking in air, then bobbing like an inner tube across the water.

As the truck swerved, he felt someone lightly touch his leg. *Barbara* he smiled. He reached out and felt fur. Disappointed, he flung the paw away, and Skidboot whined. Too bad he couldn't put the dog to work, David mused. Someone was going to have to pay for all the damage.

CHAPTER EIGHT

Cowboy vs. Dog

It wasn't really the dog's fault. Nearly grown by now, he'd run rampant for over a year, with David stifling his instincts out of respect for Barbara -- Skidboot was her dog. But he'd racked up so much damage that their fragile budget was shattered. Problems seemed to heap up exponentially, along with David's temper.

"What's this hell hound gonna do next?"

Next always turned out more baffling, more insidious, and more destructive than before.

Next happened one day when the dog followed its native cattle herding instincts, unfortunately, with someone else's cattle. Texas ranchers traded farm machinery back and forth, might be in debt to one another for an advance on a new heifer, or, even occasionally, borrow trucks. But cattle were sacred as a bank account. Grazing idly out in a field, a herd represented investment, and no one could or would interfere with another rancher's investment. Skidboot continued to break the rules.

One day as David tucked a horseshoe up to a steady position, a cavalry of cattle exploded over the hillside, heading for the gully.

"What the hell!" a voice yelled. Behind them, the furry rustler yapped and darted, nipping at hooves, keeping the herd fast but orderly. In cattle country, running off pounds of hamburger was like scattering fifty dollar bills to the wind. A fat beef cow sold by the pound for up to $3,000, which made Skidboot's juvenile cattle rustling serious business.

"Skidboot, you fool, get over here!" Alert, shaking with nervous energy, Skidboot froze. Blue sky hung peacefully, the sun rippled like taffy. A slight breeze blew butterflies in circles and everywhere, the earthy waft of manure drifted on the wind. Finally, the cattle settled back into the lazy rhythms of a sunny day.

David had lunged after the dog so violently that he probably lost a pound or two himself, and then he noticed something worse—a monstrous Brahman bull grazing isolated under a tree fifty-yards away. Skidboot followed his gaze and sprang toward it. David yelled, running after. The bull sniffed, head up, its back hump trembling. Pendulous ears gave it the look of a nun in full habit, drooping eyes half-shielded by twin wimples. Its neck wattle rippled like seaweed. Looks aside, a 2,300-pound bull takes its time making decisions, and this one switched in and out of interest, black tail flicking its white haunches, slightly bored, yet also alert. A peculiar import from India, the Brahman thrived in Texas due to its placid temperament, heat resistance and an astonishing, rubbery hide so naturally oily that it repelled Texas bugs, including mayflies, stoneflies, nits, mosquitoes, blackflies, horsebot, blowfly, and more.

Skidboot snapped around its hooves, trying to get a response, but the bull's interest flickered in and out, like a weak porch light. When it finally perked up, Skidboot's DNA whispered, *this bull can be herded.* It was the first normal behavior Skidboot had shown, and David, who had just about given up on him, rekindled. Even the most ornery horse had dignity, something the dog sorely lacked. And up until today, he suspected that Skidboot might be, well, insane. That is, if a dog *could* be insane. *And, if a dog really is insane, how can you tell?*

But now, actual herding! Skidboot snapped to as the bull lowered horns broad as a wagon bed and sharp as razor points. A man could imagine their impact and stay clear. But the dog, lacking vision, was right on the bull, only seconds away from getting kebabbed.

Skidboot barked. Down tilted the horns.

He barked again, and the bull looked confused.

"Skidboot! Get over here!" David caught' Skidboot's back leg and pulled him, snarling, skidding, paws planted, downhill. The bull shook itself and resumed grazing, bemused by all the commotion. It lost interest quickly.

The day was still fine as David threw open the truck door, blue sky outlining the twisting shape of the dog. A harsh slam of the door, and he locked it from the outside, trapping Skidboot inside. His canine Houdini could sneak out of anything they'd devised so far. He keyed the door shut and faced Skidboot through the glass, as Skidboot's eyes widened with excitement. *I love this man.*

Just to let him know, Skidboot whimpered, pawed the window, and pressed his nose to the glass, a dark olive that dragged a film down the pane as he sank back onto the seat. The two stared at each other, David trying to read the dog's gaze, the dog whimpering. Then he turned and pawed the wheel, like driving. Then he threw another look at David.

"I suggest you tell Lassie there to gun it up and drive it home," said his neighbor, who'd heard the ruckus and now watched his cattle amble slowly back up the hill. It would take another day's grazing to make up their lost weight. In a land devoid of amenities, in a harsh world of privation and risk, people had to collaborate to get along, and such unions, sprung from need or friendship, depended on reputation. Reputation was nine-tenths of interaction, and David feared that his was suffering. It wouldn't be long before clients stopped calling. No one wanted a farrier with a demon dog.

David flushed. He'd never raised an infant before, but the stigma of this one's bad behavior stuck to him, *trapped* him, making him unable to move around freely. Now he knew how young mothers must feel stuck at home. The best he could do was to leave the dog locked in the truck and hope it matured.

Sorry, it'll never happen again. Apologies all the time! Once again, mopping up after Skidboot. It didn't seem right that a Blue Heeler, the premier breed of the cattle running dogs, should be so dithering useless.

It wasn't really the dog's fault. For weeks now, Skidboot's every move had a true purpose, and that was to *get the man's attention.* His teeth had just come in, so when he attacked a stuffed toy, it had meaning, a message, *look, look at me!* He found life with the cat upsetting, the thing wanted to cuddle and claim attention from *his people*. Skidboot would stare at the cat as if it were a rattler, eyes drilling, and then begin to yap. The cat, startled, arched and hissed, and then they were off, Skidboot straining to wriggle from David's grip, the cat skidding across the floor. Skidboot chewed David's hands to escape, until he couldn't hold on any more. Skidboot envied the horses David handled, the ones he would sooth with his voice, but right now, Skidboot was thirty pounds of potential, cocked as a pistol, and he had to catch the cat. *Sure, he nipped at people, chickens, cattle, stuffed toys and those strange chickens with blue feathers, the peacocks...that's what cattle dogs did.* Everyone yelled at him, but when he got David's scent, smelled his boots, his lariat ropes, his piggin' strings, the only thing he could do was attack them and chew them up. David's historic Willie Nelson Yamaha guitar, found in a barn, restrung, polished and doted over, was now festooned with bite marks. Worse, by the time Skidboot had worn off puppyhood, he was fast and tricky, and his favorite pastime was whimpering at the door to go outside. *Outside* shone like gold, *outside* was his destination, his place to mark, to pursue, to play! David would stride over to the door, open it a crack, and let him slide through like a shadow, and when Skidboot was finished, David actually expected him to come back.

"Skidboot! Get in here!" And every time, David set off at a fast clip to catch the astonished dog, trying to herd him into a corral, or into a blind alley behind the barn, like trying to capture a light beam. He'd be one place then another, fast as a split atom, leaving David hopping around and hopping mad.

Calves excited Skidboot to no end. Calves, loose skinned, loose limbed, galloped around as if wearing pajamas. He *loved* calves. Horses, too. Especially the one that kicked him silly and nearly broke his neck. This drove David even *more* crazy, since he had to drive Skidboot to the vet's *and* pay for it. Meanwhile, Barbara drove off to work every morning after an early snuggle with her dog, while Skidboot would whimper and roll his eyes and look fetchingly over Barbara's shoulder at David. And David got more and more frustrated, knowing the day ahead would echo with the shriek of startled chickens, the thunder of running livestock, the crash of upended trash barrels, and the neighbors, reluctantly dropping by to complain. For his part, Skidboot had something to say but no one was listening. A family like this might drive a dog mad.

CHAPTER NINE

Rodeo Dreams Die Hard

Being so nervous was unseemly behavior for a rodeo champion. It distressed him but it kept happening. He unfolded to his 6'4" height, perched his hat brim square and gazed at himself. No reason a man like himself — and he glanced again — couldn't do himself proud.

The lasso tricked around his wrist, tightening when he pulled it, but firm, the way he liked it. The poly rope meant that it wouldn't stretch. Meticulous, he reviewed his throw, seeing the rope loop out toward the speeding calf, visualizing success. He'd capture the calf the minute it burst out of the gate, then wrestle it down and secure it with the piggin' string. He smiled briefly, remembering how he'd threatened to tie up Skidboot with the piggin'.

He checked the neck rope, to make sure it circled around behind the horse, ready to keep the calf taut on the line. Then the jerk line. A jerk line helps the roper control his horse while he's running toward the calf. The jerk line is fastened to the bit then threads backwards through a pulley near the saddle. The jerk line also pulls on the horse's bit, causing it to stop.

He adjusted his height into the saddle, feeling its familiar curves. "You might as well sit in a shovel," Mark Twain complained about the American saddle, cursing the man who invented it. But David had worn his to perfection, had no complaints, and felt as comfortable in it as in the seat of his truck.

Maybe today would be the big win, he thought. With cheers from the crowd as Hank sped to victory, taking them both to the National Finals.

A serious competitor, David Hartwig. But like coffee gone cold, he felt his dedication cooling. The loudspeaker blared. Time to back into the box, urging Hank uncomfortably backwards, keeping to the left side of the chute. Once in tight, he'd nod and someone would throw open the chute. Then the calf would speed out.

He ran the steps through his mind, hands itching. First, his horse was seasoned, ready to go. *Quick, with big stops, lots of pull.* He trusted the horse, all thousand pounds. He'd have to spur Hank out of the box without breaking the barrier, a rope strung in front of the box attached to the rope loosely dangling around the calf's neck. When the calf skids midway out from the chute, it releases the roper to gallop after. The distance between David and the calf is called the score. And the time it takes for the calf to travel the distance of the score is the "get out." Techniques differed, but in North Texas, they played "caught as caught can" which meant tying down the calf however possible, as long as the calf is still harnessed by the rope. Then followed the traditional, if somewhat brutal, flipping the calf through the air to thud on the ground to be tied and then wait for six seconds for the big win.

The familiar routine flashed through his mind. His stomach heaved. The hot sun nudged along his neck, a long burn, sweltering his ears. The air vibrated with flash and sound, snapping bandanas, hats waving, boots stomping the brazen cry of a western band. He loved the wild tumult of Texas tie-down roping, his thing.

Riding next, from Quinlan, Texas, we have David Hartwig!

The crowd murmured encouragingly, not yet a roar, as David's hands clutched the reins. Hank tensed beneath him, and David braced for the ride of his life. The calf squeezed into the chute and David nodded to the gate operator, *ready.*

But no one could be ready for what happened next. The gate banged open, the calf bolted into the arena, and out of nowhere, a streak of mottled blue and black raced into the box and latched onto the skid boot Hank wore on his fetlock. Behind the blue streak raced Russell, yelling *"no, no no, Skidboot, no!!*

Skidboot? David hardly formed the thought when his horse reared and smashed him into the barrier, grunting, panting as the crowd gasped in surprise. Up, up, over the barrier, the horse was on its last hooves when David slammed against the steel rail, jamming his right leg straight into the metal clutch. In horrifying slow motion, it kept getting worse, a deadly ballet gone wrong. The horse staggered, keeled over, crushing David. Below him, Skidboot growled and gnawed at the skid boot, clamped on it like an angry alligator.

"Ladies and gentlemen, let us *pray* this ends well!" The announcer was juggling his mike in place, the crowd keening in anxiety. A neon green clown shot into the arena, distracting Hank as he staggered to his feet, dragging David, limp and unconscious, out of the saddle. As the clown closed in and dove for the horse's reins, a final convulsion bucked David through the air. He landed with a thud, shattered as a clay pigeon.

"I do not *believe* what is happening!" The announcer waved toward the medical crew galloping across the field. The stretcher flipped out, arms hoisted David in and swiftly carted him away. Out cold, David knew nothing of the next few minutes when Skidboot, whether prompted by guilt or showmanship, did the unthinkable.

"Will ya look at *that!*" The crowd, tuned to any new possibility, buzzed. Barbara gazed astonished. Russell's anger suddenly drained away at what he saw. The rodeo clowns stared, huge mittens hanging idly at their sides.

In front of a thousand people, Skidboot pranced, leading the subdued horse back into the arena by its reins. Gone was the mischief, the growling, the snapping, the tugging. The dog, taut with zeal, guided the horse over to the nearest pair of hands, who took the horse away.

In a breath, the crowd roared. Applause, hoots, horns, and the music struck up even as David shook himself to and looked around. They were applauding him and, he realized with a shock, Skidboot, too. The demon dog who had caused the trouble was now sharing the moment.

He moaned. Barbara clutched his hand and Russell bent near. The only one who stayed away, and rightly so, was Skidboot, who seemed to understand David's unspoken vow of vengeance, *I'll settle with you later.*

After the excitement of the arena, lying in bed nursing a broken leg, hammered ribs and a bruised elbow seemed a relief, a time without stress or recrimination, a time to gaze vacantly at the morning light filtering through, listen to a mockingbird in the oak tree, to dream and to drift. Then responsibility nagged him. He should go see how Hank was after the fetlock attack. Horses, skittish under the best circumstances, didn't react well to drama.

Out of nowhere, a weight hit his leg, and he groaned. Skidboot planted both paws on the cast, bright eyes inquiring. The dog vibrated with nervous energy, just having him in the room felt like an active fault line. Why couldn't the dog be still?

"Skidboot, get offa me!" In a flash of black and blue, Skidboot landed on the floor in a tangle of claws, vibrating himself off to the corner where he sat staring at David, every muscle quivering.

"What do you *want?*" Everyone needed something from him, Barbara to be left alone, Russell *not* to be left alone, the neighbors next door to straighten out their mixed cattle herds, the credit cards to be paid. On and on. He sighed, hitting the pillows.

"You ok?" Barbara poked her head in, curly hair tucked behind her ear. *She is the prettiest thing.* David forgot how he'd yelled and cussed at her the other day, angry about the details of training and roping. Or how, in return, she refused to take his calls while at work, seeing him as low priority. This pained David, caused him to — briefly — sulk.

Light slatted through the blinds, striping the beige walls, curling around the wall photos of Russell as a baby and the calendar with the dates crossed off.

"Today is Russell's parent-teacher conference." Barbara adjusted her purse, primed to go. "I'll call and tell them you're sick." He frowned.

"All right, then, that you're injured."

Maybe you could go for a change, he's your son. David immediately regretted the thought, but sometimes, he felt like he did everything, while she just trotted off to a peaceful workplace. *Well, not that peaceful.* He had to be honest.

Neither of them ever mentioned "bankruptcy," but they were circling around it like driving in a full parking garage. How did they cut it so close with two adult incomes?

"We are coasting downhill," Barbara frowned. "And with you laid up, there's no leeway. Any ideas?"

In later years, David would say "I didn't plan my life out, my life planned me." Yet fate aligned itself with faith, which is something no one can plan. You have to sit tight until it comes to you.

He sighed, rolled over, hollered at the shut door and surprised himself in the bureau mirror, a monster of bandages and bruises, with a black eye and a welter of tiny cuts.

"I want that dog gone!"

Hearing David's voice, Skidboot quivered at the edge of the bed, and David couldn't shake the idea that he wanted something. He leaned toward David, looking like a dog in a high wind, nose stretched out in front, ears wiggling, every quivering inch of him completely worked up, as usual.

"Shoo!" Skidboot stared at him. David stared back. Neither blinked. Suddenly, the lights went off.

Damn, David thought. *Unpaid bill again.*

He couldn't blame Barbara, and besides, she wasn't there anyway. The dog was hopeless, and just as David tried to hobble out of bed, the doorbell rang, reminding him that, like flies in the buttermilk, things could only get worse.

CHAPTER TEN

Chicken Killer

But no, it was only Art Shipley holding something bulky, probably condolence food. Art and his wife were fine folks, and he'd probably brought over something tasty. David gladdened at the sight of whatever it might be. Covered dishes defined country living, filled in where income left off, and were the calling cards of Texas homemakers. David smiled, remembering the last covered dish event at the local grange. Hennie Patterson was the main contestant, a woman so versed in cooking that any compliment, such as "that was a mighty fine dish," produced not a "thank you," but an instant segue into the ingredient list.

"You take one cabbage, cut it fine. You sauté one onion, cut it fine. You mix up two cans tomato paste with water…." And so on. To compliment a salad only sparked up another litany.

"You take one Bibb lettuce, dismantle it, wash and chop. You get pecans and brown 'em in the oven. You take a garden tomato, maybe a yellow "sunburst" and slice it in coins…"

The vision lingered as he shuffled toward the door.

"Hey, Art." He said. "Sorry, there's no light."

Art peered in, then stood back, holding something out.

David narrowed his gaze just to be sure. The dead chicken looked like a weird door prize given away at the high school Halloween Bazaar. He blinked, unsure of what he was seeing.

"Um, Art, we don't do much cooking here...not lately."

The man coughed, embarrassed. "This here's not a gift, son, it's a dead chicken and it's one of mine. I think that dog of yours mighta killed it."

It struck David hard. Anger, followed by a surge of vindication. Sure, he was angry but right now, the universe had opened up a way for him to divest himself. One less dog, a lot more happiness. Just thinking about it made him smile.

"Something funny, Dave?" Art seemed annoyed, a seamed, weathered man who ran horses and occasional sheep, and who raised a gaggle of laying hens for breakfast eggs and occasional Sunday chicken dinner. He and the Hartwigs seldom interfered with each other, a neighborly relationship, up until now.

Skidboot barked, staring at the chicken, then barked at David. *Look, look there.*

Every dog responds to tone, and it only took Skidboot a second to realize that David, the man he was trying to get through to, now threatened him. Anger, dark and ominous, burst into the dog's consciousness. He whined, dropped his nose in submission, then, gripped by another idea, rolled his eyes fetchingly at David, longing up at him from under wiry brows, shooting him special glances. David stared back, furious and challenging. In the dark, Hartwig man and Hartwig dog tussled back and forth, the dog wanting something, hanging on to its own worth, struggling to win, or to communicate, or maybe he just wanted a chicken bone, who knew?

CHAPTER ELEVEN

Russell's Rescue

Russell ducked out the back door to escape the ruckus. Seemed lately like everything turned sour, starting with David then ending up with his mom. He dragged a stick through the loose dirt of the yard, staring out at the darkened night of Texas. *The stars at night are big and bright, deep in the heart of Texas...*The children of one generation couldn't begin to understand the world of another--the arguing, loving, reprimanding, and unfathomable behavior of parents. Vast stretches of rye grass, chaparral, and cheatgrass breezed out there in the dark, another thing no one could understand. The horizon stretched to infinity, or at least to Dallas, an idea that warmed him because it led him to his beloved grandparents, David's Ma and Pa. Just thinking of them, he felt rock solid, able to float over the daily tide of discouragement. Life in Dallas seemed unified, sensible, and happy, a place where the lights stayed on and no one bickered. His Grandma and Grandpapa made his world feel better.

A faraway bark told him that Skidboot was locked up in the woodshed again, which suited Russell fine. He was tired of the frantic flurry of paw steps always rampaging after him, of the cold nose and the huge energy. Skidboot barked again, short, needy, demanding.

Russell yelled, "No Skidboot, you go away!" He wanted some privacy, not to have to deal with Skidboot again. Russell for a moment felt the dark fury of the bully, the perpetrator, the brutish force of the aggressor over something smaller, weaker, and unable to speak. *Like me,* he realized with a start. That's how he felt at school these days, pushed around.

He scuffed his boots, disturbing a horned toad that froze in the flashlight beam and dove into the soil, only it's eyes showing, fixed and bright. Every current of life force in the tiny reptile called for quiet. Maybe Russell could learn something from a Texas horned toad, the art of camouflage and mind control. So the two cooperated, the toad lying still as winter and Russell, even though he knew it was there, pretending ignorance. He strolled by and both of them were relieved.

Studious and extremely bright in every subject, Russell teetered between admiration for David's love of the rodeo circuit and his own more academic nature. One seemed to circumvent the other. If he chose rodeo life, it would oddly empower him, like a dam that forces a flow of water in an unnatural direction. Right or wrong, directing the channel gave him a sense of being grown up. After all, how many ways to Sunday had his parents gotten it wrong?

On the weekend, he'd end up in Dallas with his grandparents, waiting to be picked up by his birth father. Sometimes he felt like a UPS parcel, going from one place to another, only to return back again. So it went, one week in Quinlan and the weekend elsewhere. Quinlan had backwater schools. He should be learning more.

"Salutatorian!" His grandparents glowed with the pride of his achievements. Everyone rolled with pride when it came to Russell, the lone youngster in the group of adults. He guessed he deserved it, his grades certainly were outstanding. Junior high school beset even the most stalwart, leaving them indecisive. Since Russell was generally obedient, his efforts to change often led him right back around to what he was supposed to do.

He was fed up with country living, fed up with Quinlan and all the jokes about it. Then he smiled, remembering one in particular.

"You born in Quinlan?"

"No, but I got here as soon as I could."

He grinned, then frowned again. Distracted and daydreaming, he walked around the corner, never imagining that he was heading into trouble of a different order, something more tangible, more frightening, than anything yet.

Inside the house, David and Barbara were head to head, trying to figure out bills, Russell, work prospects, and how to divide up the chores. David thought Barbara was too hard on the boy, Barbara thought David was too soft. For a child of divorce, Russell was surrounded by adults, who circled around, issued rules, laws, declarations and advice, who came up with game plans spilling over with conflicting moves. Agree to disagree seemed to be the style.

Suddenly, Skidboot broke into a round of intense barking, decibels rising in a frantic, noisy pandemonium ranging wildly up the scale of canine vocals. By the time he hit howl, Both Barbara and David were so irritated they turned in unison.

'Skidboot, *shut up!*"

"He don't like being locked up," David said. "He's mad, but we can be madder. We have to make him learn."

Russell had been outside later than usual. Dusk had drawn softly into evening, and as he walked around behind the barn, he kicked through the hay, while listening to the horses munch and breathing in the night. He mused to himself, thinking over the day's events in school. Here he had privacy and could think his own thoughts. He watched the stars poke through the dark sky, one after another, drawing down the night. Then he heard a chilling sound, part snort, part growl—a hair raising emanation that shot out of the dark, unidentifiable, horrific and scary. Like the noises he'd heard in that werewolf movie at the cinema last month. The same guttural trapped sound, as if a huge force was pushing itself up out of the ground. Russell struggled backwards, barely able to see in the dim star shine. He flipped on his flashlight again, and waved it—*my light sabre--* in the direction of the sound. The guttural sound burst out again, a sound that seemed horribly familiar, and would have caused a hunter to flip off his gun's safety *that very minute* to prepare to shoot down a wild pig.

The javalina is North America's most grotesque feral throwback, a misshapen peccary humped up at the shoulders like an economy buffalo, leaving its outsized head hanging straight down, dragged there by the weight of its tusks. A misfit beast, with teeth too long and legs too short, it made up for its shortcomings with the nasty temperament of a yak and the remarkable action of tusks that would self-sharpen whenever the mouth opened or closed. Hunted by sharpshooters, dreaded by homeowners, the hairy, musty, dung-rolled javalina often hid in basements and carports of the unsuspecting to wreak havoc, a danger to anything in its path. People could be wounded. Worse, the javalina typically herded with its kind, which meant if you saw one, there were probably more out there, circling around.

In this case, something must have stirred it up, since it usually sheltered after dark. Barks of outrage, challenge and anger collided into a howl that rose up into the night as Skidboot threw himself against the confines of the wooden dog pen. Later, Skidboot would reflect, in that way that a dog *could* reflect, that he did not deserve to be penned. Everyone else would reflect, in a storytelling way, that maybe it was the poor fencing material, or maybe a loose wire, but really, however it happened, the dog just flew over the fence.

"Hog!" David hollered. As he limped through the dark, he bumped over a water bucket, battled exposed pipes, kicked paint cans and collided seriously into an angular metal thing that felt like a wheelbarrow. He disentangled himself and limped faster. Up ahead, outlined by the glow of a flashlight, he saw the hog, forelegs planted, mouth like a bagpipe in a full, ear-splitting squeal.

Squeal didn't describe it, he told people later. Squeal is more of a cartoon sound, like the Three Little Pigs, rather than this splintering shriek. The sound was like framework ripping at a construction site, an anarchy of splintered boards, the attack call of a hog that meant business. David shuddered, his game leg like cardboard, bending in all the wrong places.

Still yards away, David paused a minute and let out a sudden roar, a sound so loud it startled himself, the javalina, and especially Russell, who panicked to think that hogs were now stampeding from the rear. The hog gathered itself up like an accordion, then shot toward Russell, hoping to make a quick finish of things and get away from the foul smell of humans.

The next moment fractured into a chaos of sound as Barbara screamed and rushed toward her son, David roared as he swung his crutch at the feisty hog, then lost his balance and toppled over. The hog turned from Russell to the downed man and sped at him, tusks thrust low.

Then it was over. A streak of mottled black, a flash of fangs, a dog that leaped at the hog's neck, bit deep, then jumped back, barking up a frenzy. The hog had no sense of what happened only that something *had* happened. Something that meant *retreat.* Pain and fear drove it back into the dark, away from this crazy barnyard of screaming humans.

"How the heck..." Barbara rushed to Russell, and they all turned and marveled at Skidboot, a Houdini whose dark arts had helped him through an unopened pen. The woodshed, obviously, couldn't hold him.

"Can he sleep with us tonight?" *About time* Skidboot thought, questioning David, even though Russell and Barbara were hugging and tugging at him, smooching him, cuddling, complimenting. A straight line of sight shot toward David's eyes.

"Maybe this dog's a pointer," he said. "A hunter."

David had to break gaze, as there were calls to make and bills to settle, and this staring contest with a dog got on his nerves. Skidboot kept facing the spot where David had been for a minute after, then finally dropped his head and began to lick his coat. Up, then down, then up again, delicately, finding precision in the small damp trail of tongue against fur. The dog was intent on his work and deliberately did *not* look at David again. At least not for a while.

CHAPTER TWELVE

Is he a dog or what ...?

Morning dawned on a household so quiet that even the mice tiptoed. A house that sucked up silence from the surrounding hills and from the pale, clueless sky. Silence settled like dust, filling the corners and soothing David. With Barbara at work and Russell at school, David was left to flip a lariat around, trying out a new brand of polyester rope to see whether it had slippage. He hoisted the noose against his boot to give it a pull, but then his crutch clattered to the floor and knocked over his coffee. Premium blend splattered on his Levi's. He sighed, daubing them dry. He'd made Russell breakfast and lunch, usually a satisfying task but today he felt irked because the Raisin Bran was short of raisins and they were out of milk. A bowl of dried cereal with tap water seemed a pitiful start to the day. He needed to make a grocery list, yet he just sat there, silent, brooding, staring at his pencil.

His thoughts zigzagged back and forth, one telling him that the dog was *not* insane, that on two occasions he'd shown rational behavior, once leading the horse back after David's accident, then last night, attacking the javalina. Lurking in that furry mayhem were the seeds of instinct, like concern for his family, loyalty, even decision making. It didn't seem right to let a possible intelligence go to waste. Why, the dog had even taken to imitating him, limping after David with identical, mincing steps, a real sideshow.

Rudy Hartwig, David's Dad, had said to him on many occasions, "always travel light." David himself had translated that to mean "make the most of what you have," which in this case, was an oddball Blue Heeler who thought he was a human. David chugged back a glass of water. He sat on the sofa and tossed a baseball from hand to hand, thinking. Fate rested in the final toss, as in *will I* or *will I not?* Back and forth, the ball plopped from one hand to another. On the final toss, he lost his grip because of a searing pain in his leg. The ball fumbled out of his hand and rolled under the sofa — gone.

Just then a ruckus struck up under the sofa, flushing the dust balls into a swirl on the floor. A black nose poked out, retreated, then poked out again as Skidboot cautiously emerged. The dog had the ball in his mouth. He planted himself in front of David, panting, with that same signature gaze — a hypnotist to his subject.

Now? Now? Now could he play, *now, now?* Skidboot nosed the ball up and down, as in *look, look!*

David sighed. *What a show off.* A boaster, a beggar, an annoying blitz in their orderly lives. David mused, watching the dog. His nature was to fix things. If rattlers slithered out to the barn, he'd pitchfork them. If mice invaded, he'd design a trap. If the calves had nits, he'd dip them. So why the delay with Skidboot? He couldn't figure it, but knew it had to do with him being Barbara's dog and respecting her ownership. She'd had pets all her life growing up in California, and she'd formed a tight bond with this dog, pesky or not. When she got home from work, Skidboot lay waiting for her, tucked under her horse trailer. If his paw had a thorn, or he had the sniffles, he headed straight to Barbara for pampering. David respected that, but courtesy time was just about over. It was time for something else.

David reached for the ball and slapped it into his hand.

"Yes sir, I will!" he said, narrowing his eyes at Skidboot, who quivered in front of him like a pile of springs, nearly shaking, ready to go. People say a dog is like a child that never grows up. David was about to prove that one wrong.

CHAPTER THIRTEEN

Leash Law

The day had started normal enough. A few pillows gnawed, one toy demolished. Amazing that the Hartwigs still gave him so many toys, which was a *happy thing*. The stuffed rabbit lay mangled in a heap of corduroy and polyester, after which Skidboot smacked his way through breakfast. He was just about to gnaw Russell's leather belt when David's shadow fell over him. Outside, morning light silvered in, and when David rose up to his full height and dangled the skid boot in front of him, Skidboot, *the dog,* got so excited, so hysterical, that he forgot to look up at David's face.

Which would have terrified him. It was screwed up into a mask of pure determination, a gritty, even hateful look, one purely different from the face he usually wore in the morning, which looked easygoing and friendly.

But not now.

David glared at him, then waggled the leather skid boot, which made *the canine* Skidboot delirious. He locked on like a pit bull, growling, pulling and eyeing the rope David had tied to the railing. *Rope practice, yes!* Then David stretched tall toward the upper cupboard, and balancing on his crutches, he brought Skidboot's favorite treat, milk bones, after which he hobbled like a crippled thing outside to the corral, where he stumbled around to set up a folding chair. This seemed to Skidboot, well, uninteresting. Maybe they'd rope calves? He didn't see how David could walk using that funny wooden support. Skidboot decided not to think about that, as it prompted some bad feeling in him. He didn't know why.

So David had sat there. One man, one chair, in the middle of a corral outside of Quinlan, Texas. He fiddled with the loop on the rope, moving it up and down, tightening it, trying it thoughtfully, slowly, with purpose. But where were the calves, the dog wondered?

"I don't like you, Skidboot. Never have. Probably never will. But you live here and while you do, you're gonna understand a few things."

The voice, silky and low, bothered Skidboot. It didn't sound right, it had a nasty ring to it. He moved back and away, on full alert. But when David reached into his pocket and pulled out his favorite toy, the gnawed-up skid boot, Skidboot relaxed. *Yes, time to play!* He bounded into the corral and hauled to a stop by the boot, ears pitched forward to pick up the drift of things. He locked onto the skid boot, dangling from David's hand.

David twirled his lasso once, casually, and the noose landed with a light bounce in the dirt in the middle of the corral, where it lay like a huge eye, ready to wink. Then he casually lobbed the leather skid boot into the perimeter, another bull's eye. The dog, electrified, saw his skid boot land.

"Ok, now, " David had commanded, unnecessary permission to a dog already launched, about to explode onto his prey, a toy that reeked with the most delicious scent of horse, and of David, and best of all, of that incredible, reaffirming aroma of Skidboot *himself.*

Just as he snapped at the boot, the lasso snapped around his neck and stopped him. He heard David spinning out in low, silky tones a constant string of insults, like *you ruined me, dog,* and *you're gonna learn 'WHOA' if it's the end of you.* At the end of each sentence, he jerked the rope, causing involuntary agitation on the dog's part. Then, to Skidboot's horror, David pushed himself down on top of the dog, flattening him, waiting instinctively for the squirming and hyper-panting to stop. The moment hung between heartbeat and coma, between predator and prey, between master and slave. There was nothing or no one — not Russell, not Barbara, not the SPCA — to rescue the one or dissuade the other.

If left up to professional trainers, the human/dog bond might be encouraged in a different way. Standard obedience exercises take place, both on and off leash, with an objective to teach a dog to heel, to go, to sit, stay or come while working through behavioral difficulties. Their aim is to "realize the dream of what such a relationship can be" by employing "a philosophy of praise, fairness and discipline, set against a background of patience, repetition and dedication." Had David any knowledge of, or ability to pay for professional training, he would be entitled, at the end of the session, to an extensive written report on how what he was currently doing was all wrong.

David whispered, *God help me do this one,* as Skidboot's new regimen began, hesitantly at first, seeking the next step based not on anything he actually knew, but just on instinct. And one instinct led to the other, until, with a final pull on the rope, David nearly cut off the dog's air. Skidboot froze, his eyes glued on David.

"No more skid boots." David jerked the rope again.

"No more trouble!" He ignored Skidboot's eyes, which were begging for mercy.

Power, dominance, alpha status and life itself hung in the balance. Without precedent or guidelines, David simply *knew* that first you ruled, then you gentled. He'd established his dominance and now it was time for something else. He ran his hand along Skidboot's head, feeling the raised bump of his forehead, the long thin nose, the surprised brows with a few light hairs sprouting out. Then he ran his fingers up and down the snout, feeling the skin quiver under his touch. No snapping or growling. Hardly even a breath. Only silence.

Good!

Then David firmly rubbed along Skidboot's back, making sure to raise his hand before repeating the motion, not wanting to run counter to the line of the fur. Again, not a tremor, the dog frozen as a statue.

Calmly, he reached down and untied the hog loop binding Skidboot's legs. Skidboot lay inert. Only his muscles quivered.

Good!

It was all instinct. Since childhood, he'd had such instincts, and they usually turned out right. If someone said "no" he'd ignore it. He never accepted anyone else's version of anything. As a child, he'd squall and scream, throwing one tantrum after another because he *wanted things his way*, a boy who turned to a man with an obstinate streak, what others might call *eccentric*, to put it kindly. Eccentric meant he usually failed to pursue normal, everyday behavior, *not unlike this dog*.

Right now, he'd invented the new normal. No more screaming at this dog, swearing at it up and down, threatening death. That debate was over. Now it was time to get down to work, although *what kind of work* still remained unclear. David, like a sculptor, was feeling his way around the block of stone, trying to get the dim outline of the future, tapping with his hammer, tracing the path, about to take the first chip.

With bullheaded precision he knew that the only way to train a horse was to scare it to death. Not with brutality, but with extreme, extrovert behavior, like jumping around on one foot with a handful of feathers or singing off key while making faces. If he could get the horse's 100% attention, then he could put the horse into a state of complete neutral. When in neutral, it didn't have to make its own decision, be fearful of predators or get jittery about shadows, low-hanging branches, gopher holes, rattlers or windstorms. It would idle away, almost inert, ready to do what a man wanted it to do. The minute you lost control, the horse's eyes would bulge outward, startled as a sand crab. It would search frantically around for danger, scenting the air, bucking, shying at any shadow. By then, all was lost.

If David knew anything, it was how to keep an animal frozen to attention.

He looked down and saw that Skidboot was still, not even a tremble, although he saw the sensation rippling beneath his fur, both agitation and excitement. As Skidboot lay there, his mouth curled *just slightly* into a whisper of a smile, it was almost as if this was something Skidboot *wanted*, not a dreaded punishment.

"Get up!" David stood tall over the dog, saw his shadow ripple as Skidboot sprang to his feet, waiting.

What? He didn't expect this kind of attention, this quickly.

Good boy, he thought, but didn't give Skidboot the satisfaction of his sentiments, not yet.

Any dog can fetch, David believed. But this dog had to follow *all* the rules.

CHAPTER FOURTEEN

Good Dog!

Then nothing much happened. David had three calves to deliver over to Sheffield's and needed to pick up some tackle odds and ends from town. He'd promised Barbara dinner out that Friday night so he made sure his shoeing was finished in time. He'd avoided Skidboot the next day, not for any particular training reasons, but just because he hadn't thought up the next step. Not yet.

Barbara had the next good idea. As Skidboot ranged around the house, flicking his tail, eyes darting, looking for something to gnaw, she grabbed a pair of David's knee-high white athletic socks, the kind with a double blue stripe along the top and tied them in a knot in the middle. Skidboot perked up, one eyebrow raised. *Now what?*

She dangled the sock foot and Skidboot, like White Fang of the Klondike, flashed through the air and chomped on the sock, pulling, gnawing, flailing to devour, destroy and denature the flopping thing. She let go. The sock-and-dog dervish spun though the living room, scattering magazines, barely missing the glass figurine, tumbling over a wastebasket and raveling up the carpet into shaggy peaks. No one could believe how many directions Skidboot could spin, and the show went on for half an hour. Finally, wrung out, Skidboot panted in place, the long sock draped over his head.

"You know, if we just clap..." she hesitated, feeling silly. Then she clapped. David clapped. Russell shouted, *yay*, and Skidboot, used to hearing only yells and curses, stared at them, eyes wide.

Skidboot, GOOD DOG! They jigged in place, clapped like bells, yelled *hoo-rah* and *yay* and with terrible impatience, waited for him to either start again or fall down in a faint.

Skidboot factored. He pondered the idea of applause, savored it, and then with a flip of the socks, threw himself back into a spin, beating himself side to side with the dangling toes of the sock, spinning around himself a halo of spittle, a frantic doggie vortex of agitation. After an insupportable amount of time, he simply had to stop. And when he did, they clapped again, loud and hard and yelled his name.

This gave Skidboot his first taste of cause and effect, but in a *good* way. First David, now Barbara, it made Skidboot almost dizzy. New things were going on. He couldn't wait.

CHAPTER FIFTEEN

Lending a Paw

"What are you all doing?" Russell, always observant, had picked up on the fact that instead of his parents running through the mobile home yelling and chasing the dog, Skidboot was mincing after them. In fact, Skidboot followed David around now, glued to his heels despite the fact that David made a big show of ignoring him, which was also different, and difficult, since Skidboot imitated his every move, even limping pathetically. They'd traded roles. It seemed weird.

"Nothing much, at least not yet." The subject of the dog clouded over them like a toxic smoke, smothering their natural upbeat repartee. A damper on the spirits for sure.

David couldn't figure out why he felt so grudging about this training, like it was some dark secret, some unnatural act. Dark and gloomy but also on the threshold of something. He just had to figure it out.

He hopped into the truck, noting the cup holder still had the morning's coffee, half-drunk. He'd been so preoccupied, he'd forgotten. He tossed down a swallow, but cold coffee made him unhappy.

He hollered for Russell to jump in. He wanted to show the boy a few horseshoeing tricks, particularly the part about gentling the horse. Not showing fear or anxiety was key. Why, there were tribes in the Amazon that made little shamanistic bracelets for themselves out of snakeskin, believing that it protected them from snakebite. And it generally did, because just having the bracelets made them feel safe. And the flash of fear was what panicked the snake and made it attack. No fear, fewer attacks. All animals were spooked by fear, and it was a man's responsibility, being the reasoning one, to eliminate their fear. To work with animals was easily the most sacred and most presumptuous, the most fraternal and rewarding pastime imaginable. People at one with animals lived without pretension in a world of mute dignity. David was one of them.

David caught Russell's eye and grinned. He'd been lucky with this boy, a son to him, the cutest little guy he'd ever seen at age three, and they'd been close ever since. His wife didn't want more children, thought that childbearing was hard work and was done with it. Russell was the only son he'd ever have, and he enjoyed every minute of it.

Barks, sharp, increasingly desperate, hit the truck. *Nuisance dog.*

"Ok, Skid, hop in."

Nodding sunflowers followed the truck as it chugged down the back roads through Quinlan, West Tawakoni, Tawakoni South, Able Springs and Cash. Dust billowed behind. Alongside the road, young green shoots of mixed grasses shimmered, and the brown slush of winter had hardened into ruts that bumped and jammed beneath the tires. They passed fences mended with plywood planks and a bingo hall as bullet marked and peeling as the Alamo. *Ahhh,* David thought, long legs stretched out, blue sky ahead, dotted with innocent white clouds.

An hour later, he held a hoof in his lap, hammering away on a 7-year-old Friesian gelding, a smart and desirable breed, popular in Quinlan and surrounding ranches. This one had the cuticle of an elephant. Russell might enjoy seeing it.

"Russell, want to see this?"

Russell looked a bit sulky, scuffed his boot in the dirt. "Why don't you let me shoe him? You know I can do it."

David hesitated. A frisky, nervous horse…no, this wasn't the place to begin.

"Son, you can help me a lot just by keeping an eye on things." Russell shrugged in an enormous, teenage pantomime of angst, jammed himself back into the truck and made an elaborate show of falling asleep. Hat pulled low, he dozed.

David pulled, plied and hammered. The rim, thick and overgrown, needed a big trim and to do it, he needed his other hammer. "Russell," he shouted, "hand me the hammer."

Back to the car, hunched over his work, David felt a presence behind him, reached around and felt the cold nudge of the hammer.

"Thanks, son." He continued working, but felt the eager presence still behind him. The sun was nearly at noon so the shadows had shortened, but nothing would have shortened Russell's shadow to this size. Or given it a sharp nose and four paws.

"Skidboot?" David struggled around under the weight of the hoof. The gelding shuddered, suddenly spooked. Skidboot sat impassively by, staring at David with gleaming eyes.

Unbelieving, David yelled over to Russell but could see from the slouched hat that Russell was sleeping or pretending to. Hammer? Russell sighed, rudely interrupted. Then thumbed his hat lazily back on his head, and sat up. No, he had not gotten David the hammer.

They stared at the dog, and David, in full experimental mode, ordered Skidboot to take the hammer *back* to the truck

Skidboot processed the idea of "back" as opposed to "bring me" and, slightly smiling, bent down, gummed the wooden handle and dragged it back to the truck. He paused then because jumping up with the hammer was more difficult than jumping out. But the message was clear.

Here's your hammer. What now?

CHAPTER SIXTEEN

I Had a Dream

David looked at the seat beside him and saw Skidboot, wearing dark glasses. The dog had his own seat; they were flying first class. Skidboot's dark glasses were too loose and kept sliding down, while David's own shades felt theatrical. He felt like a movie star, and he knew that these first class seats cost more than he made in a month. David sighed in contentment. Skidboot sighed too. In a few hours they'd meet a limo at the airport with a driver who held up your name so everyone could see that you had a limo.

The stewardess leaned close, offering them champagne. He didn't think Skidboot should drink but ordered one for him anyway. He could have two for himself, then. The stewardess made little pooch noises at Skidboot, who cocked an eye and stared back at her. People always picked some idiosyncratic way of communicating with his dog, either 'tsk tsk' noises, or 'oooooo' or now, like this one, little smacks. Funny, but with Skidboot, you didn't really have to say anything. Just think it.

They had duck confit and scampi, and Skidboot licked the plate clean. Dessert next, and they both hoped it was ice cream.

CHAPTER SEVENTEEN

Canine Einstein

David woke with a start. Skidboot, a star? *Oh, right, in his own horror movie,* David laughed. Still, he had a burning curiosity. Any dog that could fetch a hammer and find the phone was pretty special.

What was that...? Hot breath blew on his face, he knew it wasn't anything human. Skidboot stared at him with such intensity that David rolled out of bed, "all right, all right, let me get some coffee."

Russell, en route to school, yelled, "I want to see some new tricks today!" Skidboot wagged his tail so violently David thought the milk would spill. Maybe he'd start with a stick or two.

By noon, the sticks were flying, the dog running back and forth like all the countless eager mutts in Texas. Any dog could fetch, but David was sure this dog understood, well, English. Or at least the doggie version of it.

With the next branch sailing through midair, David commanded, "Whoa!"

Skidboot froze, one paw raised. The stick bounced invitingly. The dog quivered.

"Whoa! Do-NOT-MOVE!" More quivers, eyes glued. "Go get it!"

Skidboot flashed across the yard and in seconds had the stick. A Rhode Island Red strutted across the tarmac behind David's truck, immediately within view of the dog. One of the greatest chicken breeds of all time, its rich brown eggs brightened up many a Sunday omelet. Lately, the hen looked frayed, acted skittish, and her eggs tasted poorly, which probably had to do with the dog. Skidboot quivered around, stirring up dust, crouched to attack.

"No!" David commanded with authority.

Skidboot dropped to a crouch, gripped with terrible indecision, head swiveling from David's location to where the chicken paraded, then back again. He longed to launch a stealth attack, but slowly, his nose dropped to his paws even though his eyes stayed screwed onto the hen, dark with thoughts of death.

I been saying no to that dog for a year, David thought. *Why now? What's different?*

Every story has a turning point, and every life is a story. Skidboot, long the only human dog he knew, had turned, heading somewhere new and exciting and far beyond the practical. Shreds, rips, toys and tumult came to nothing. In fact, they came to a halt. Once mute with misunderstanding, Skidboot now, finally, understood. He was ready to work, just the way he was meant to.

The household temperature warmed to him, releasing its icy anger at his whoppers of chicken chasing and frantic barking, softening into the surprise of cooperation and the magic of number "Three." In the classics, Virgil, Caesar and Aeneas promote the occult use of three. Churches in the past had glorified the number three with triangular shapes, three organs, three towers, three doors, all dedicated to the Three of the Trinity. Mystical and mysterious, it seemed appropriate. The mystery of this dog was only beginning to show itself.

'When I count to *three* you touch that tree." Skidboot grew still as a French mime, his paw outstretched, waiting for David to *say the number*. He heard thirty, ten, four, thirteen, eleven—the numbers rattling through his brain like bids at an auction, but it was only after everyone had tired, and David's two buddies, Cal and Sip, got up to leave, that David gave in and whispered, "three."

In a flash, Skidboot's paw marked the tree.

"Gawd, look at that!"

"Now back up." Spoken lightly. Then, careful as a woman in heels, Skidboot felt the ground behind him, paw searching after paw, his eyes steady on David as he inched along.

"Now stop."

He stopped.

"Now go."

He went.

"Now stop."

He stopped.

Laughter surged. The men clapped, and Russell grinned, proud of the family dog. He'd seen their routine for the last three days, with David giving orders and the dog, ears perked, hanging on *every word.* Linguists would argue that sure, a dog could understand up to 100 specific words, command words such as "go," "stop" or a word to identify an item, such as "stick" or "ball." So could a child, only the child would go further and learn concepts, like "love" or "friendly." Eventually, the child would come to make sense of a sentence using a number of identifiable words, whereas a dog would still be stuck on the individual meanings.

"You ought to get that dog on the circuit," they all said.

What circuit? David wondered.

CHAPTER EIGHTEEN

Commando Dog

Barbara didn't compete with David, rodeo-wise. She trusted his ability to win, and he'd been on winning streaks before. In the dour, weather-beaten, tight-fisted gaggle of rodeo riders and their unhappy wives, he took pride in her restraint and whole-hearted support. She wasn't the usual rodeo wife, a disappointed woman with unmet domestic needs, who nagged her spouse, pinched up her eyes in the bright sun and tried not to see him riding, a wife who resented the circuit and who groused about the paltry pay. Instead, Barbara decided to learn some of the rodeo routines herself. Often, she would help David practice. She ducked under his occasional tongue lashing, delivered in volatile, colorful terms by a perfectionist who could swear up a steak and call down fury on any mistake. But the cloud lifted when the work was done, and he resumed his role as a rodeo rider not afraid to talk about feelings, and not afraid to show friendship, support and sensitivity.

One particularly harsh day he felt like a volcano, bubbling inside with ambition, frustration, perfectionism. He'd bellowed like Vesuvius erupting. *Everything* was wrong, why didn't she fix it, how could she…blah blah. Barbara just stood there, dumbfounded by the volley, waiting for it to subside. David roared out of the driveway, bound for a 3-day circuit, hat pulled low on his brow as the tires spun out. The last glimpse he had of his wife was of her standing unhappy by the barn gate, the wind lifting her long hair.

I shouldn't blow up like that, he thought. *Gotta do better.*

On his return, he couldn't believe what greeted him. It rose like a vision before him, odd looking, jerry-built and leaning up against the roping area as if blown there by a Northern. Yet it looked sturdy, too, and of a design he admired the minute he saw it. It huddled up against the roping area, a thing he had wanted, needed, never had the time to build for himself, and—he squinted, just to make sure he wasn't hallucinating in the hot sun—someone had built one.

A return alley.

What the…?

It was Barbara who had built it—by hand! An entire wooden return alley, stuck to the side of the corral—he was astonished. She'd made him a peace offering, a showing of love, even after his ugly yelling behavior…he felt ashamed.

While he was gone, she'd lifted, sorted, arranged, hammered and nailed the boards together, although where she found the materials, he didn't know. She probably had to measure everything out carefully, too, then get them sawn at the hardware store, then haul them back. He tried to imagine her hammering, holding the slats together, dropping nails, getting Russell to hold parts while she nailed them together. It just didn't make sense; she had no skill as a carpenter.

But there it stood, his own return alley. Other men might get a pearl snap-front western shirt or a hand-sewn leather wallet, but his wife gave him a return alley! This roundabout device set into their 150-ft. corral would soften his practice considerably; cut time off the calf's return, which would give him more good cutting and turning practice. Astonished, he stared at the contraption, feeling....loved.

"Barbara, you have got *backbone!*" he complimented, happy to see that she smiled in return. And remembering her toughness then made it easier to understand the scene that happened the next day.

He'd just driven home, turned off the key, when she flung herself out of the mobile home, yelling. Barbara was the last person he expected to yell, at least not without a hog attack or a house fire. He jammed out of the car, startled.

"I got him to lay down and crawl!"

This project had driven David wild. He couldn't seem to make Skidboot understand *crawling*. Since none of their tricks involved actual body language, only verbal language, he'd failed to convince the dog, even by falling to the floor and mock crawling, that crawling was something he should do. Skidboot might as well have been offered a Tango session, given the disinterest and his frantic eye-darting to avoid looking at David, hopelessly riddled down on the floor. *Get up sir!* he might have thought. Skidboot could not believe the ends to which this family would go. He resisted crawling. It seemed demeaning, puppy-like and servile, none of which Skidboot was.

"Look! I'll show you." To the astonishment of man and dog, Barbara flung herself into the air, and like a quarterback landing a tackle, sailed straight on top of Skidboot. Then she reached out and paddled with feet and hands stretched out, sneezing at the dusty shag carpet, Skidboot pressed underneath like a skateboard. A minute into this and Skidboot, interested in his life, lashed out in swimming-like motions, bearing up bravely under his excited load. Like some dystopian were-animal, the duo inched along, Barbara's pony tail bouncing, Skidboot's speckled tail beating out a frantic backlash underneath.

As this... *thing* pulled itself across the floor, David flew into an uncharacteristic laughing fit. He teetered into a chair, shaking with great, sucking howls, sparking Russell into even greater hilarity as he choked back his tears and giggles, as they both discovered that yes, their dog *really could crawl.*

Wiping his eyes, David wondered if he was supposed to use this dog-as-skateboard routine out in the arena? Throw himself over the dog, swim with him?

"No, look!" Barbara jumped up, crossed the room. "Skidboot, crawl!"

David's *skin* crawled as he watched Skidboot slowly lower himself to the rug, paws outspread, nuzzle thrust into the shag, eyes fixed on Barbara, and then, in a show of haunch and knobby joints, like crawling in the mud on D-Day, Skidboot pulled himself across the floor, crawling.

CHAPTER NINETEEN

Who's Top Dog?

A delicious stillness settled over the evening, broken melodically by cicadas or the liquid query of a whippoorwill. The fading daylight erased the harsh edges of the day, rubbing them into soft lavender and grey, as everything grew silent and humbled by the fine light of the first star. Those same stars had looked down on the Mexican troops that raided San Antonio, who bested the Texas rangers, who forced them to bargain for their lives with "beans for death," the selection of white beans meaning life, and black beans leading seventeen to die, and the stars overhead had blinked to hide themselves from the sight.

So much bygone history. So many lives and deaths, all for the republic of Texas. And the tide of the present kept moving, pulling the past behind it, nothing ever staying still for more than its time. And now here he was too, flowing along toward some end. Some destiny. But what kind, David couldn't tell. Then the unexpected.

"Go on, use Skidboot, I give you permission!"

Barbara hugged the dog, and Skidboot stared up at her, then at David, who thought he'd misunderstood. *She must be joking.* But no, Barbara had followed her business instincts and decided that Skidboot had entertainment potential. Sure, David's rancher friends had said so from the start, but David hadn't paid any attention. But Barbara had called the Malakoff Cornbread Festival organizers. She'd described Skidboot, his routines, and they thought it sounded fine.

Trained hell, was all David could say. One thing to have fun with a stick, another to parade it around the fairgrounds to the tune of pure ridicule. David understood the Big Win, had spend his adult years riding after it, and in his mind, the Big Win came with skill and athleticism, not by being a clown.

"What that dog's doing is extraordinary," Barbara insisted. "He has a special talent, why not share it?"

He has a special talent! David was surprised at the flare of quick jealousy. Now I'm competing with a dog! "All Skidboot does is fetch, what's so special about that?" He felt a flicker of shame. Because he knew the dog was extraordinary, but he also knew that whatever they had together depended on both of them. He would rather shoe wild horses *while they were galloping* than trot himself into an arena with a dog.

He hobbled over to his electric Yamaha, seeking solace in music. Fingers strumming, he sounded out the notes of a favorite Beatles tune, *Yellow Submarine.* Music spoke to him, no it *sang* to him, almost as much as roping, riding or even swimming.

The microwave hummed away right next to the piano, and he never turned it on without sitting down at the piano to play a quick tune. Music drew him, usually folk tunes, 'sixties standards and an occasional cowboy ditty. He seated himself, tall at the piano bench. Eyes closed, he hummed out a simple version of "Submarine" as the room fell dark around him. Lost in the tune, he failed to understand the activity at his elbow, as Skidboot wriggled up beside him. If dogs can love music, if dogs have the necessary sensor neurons delicate enough for fine hearing, then it explained Skidboot, who resisted the ability to howl and instead, delicately waved his paw, as if conducting. Head cocked, he accompanied the music for several seconds, seeking the rhythm. Then, at the crescendo, "we all live in a yellow submarine," he reached over and tapped the keys, gently. Once. Twice. David stopped. *What?*

David played a minor key, challenging Skidboot. Skidboot tapped a minor key, although not the same one. Then David tapped C-major, a white key. Skidboot pondered, then hit D, also a white key. David tapped out "Ba, ba, black sheep" on the white keys, hitting C-C-G-G-A-A-G, throwing Skidboot a smug look. *Take that!* Skidboot mused, head cocked, and for a horrifying second David thought he was going to transpose the ditty to minor keys, but the paw hovered over the black keys, then came down lightly. Then the paw stopped.

Aw, he's just counting, Of course dogs can count, all the so-called "talking dogs" were really copycat mutts who imitate human sound by dividing the words into beats. Someone says "how are you?" and the dog hears three syllable and howls back, *how-rrr – you!* Seldom actual words, the syllables only represent speech, at least enough to pass. But a *piano playing dog?* Astonishingly, Skidboot patted out three more notes, incorrect for the song but just the right beat. David shivered, as if he'd glimpsed something from another world.

CHAPTER TWENTY

Dog Launch

A week later, David stood at the corner of Terry Street and East Royal Blvd. in the town square of Malakoff, Texas, about 80 miles southeast of Dallas. Storefronts trailed crepe paper, and the jaunty booths hoisted crazy flags and sailed bouquets of balloons. David limped behind the dog, feeling disgruntled. He'd always felt sorry for carnival types, thinking they were unfortunate folks to earn such a living. And now, he was one of them.

Next, it's the Black Eye Pea Festival, David grouched. *Then the Syrup Fair.* His main interest today was to avoid bumping into anyone he knew and especially Randy Coyle, who oddly enough, he'd spotted strolling near the pickle booth with a couple of cowboy singers. David ducked behind a cornbread stand, one of many scattered around the square. No one knew why cornbread counted in Malakoff, a town actually renowned for brick making. Malakoff was the production site of light-hued bricks dyed in various shades, an elegant trick in 1904, long before people had come to expect colorful embellishment. But today, a brick making festival would be even less attended than a cornbread feed.

Malakoff also bore the notorious distinction of being named after a Russian fort from the Crimean War, but more lately, was home to a colorful wall mural painted by a local artist who featured the town citizens staring down from the wall. To some, the painted people looked more lively than the real ones. But bricks and cornbread aside, Malakoff remained a dusty, one-horse town, population less than 3,000. A puny venue.

David grimaced, his knee buckling. He still had the crutch for support and hoped that this dog deal didn't call for any kind of athletics. His imagination still failed to understand how he and Skidboot could be considered entertainment.

A portly man huffed up, his shirt hitched oddly over his pants. Sweat beaded his brow, April in Texas being griddle hot. "Mr. Hartwig," he wondered, eyeing David suspiciously until he saw the dog. "You all right, sir?" He gestured toward the leg, understanding that out here, a man could fall off a log or be born handicapped and it was purely his own business. He stared at David until David finally blurted out, "I fell off a stool playing checkers."

Russell snickered, then looked serious. "That's right, except before that, the horse fell on you at the rodeo, right?" He turned to Robert Reese, the coordinator of the Malakoff festival. "He's *real tough.*"

Reese nodded seriously. He turned to look at Skidboot.

"This here's the dog?" He bent down and gazed at Skidboot, who gazed back. "What kinda tricks can he do?"

Russell looked down at Skidboot proudly. He loved showing off his dog. He winked at Skidboot.

"Ask him yourself."

The man looked embarrassed and then upset. The boy must be making fun of him.

"No, really. Just tell him to do something."

Skidboot looked up at the circle of faces, which included his favorites, Russell and David. They had those intent looks, and he wondered what it would be today: The telephone? Counting games?

Mr. Reese softened, bent down toward Skidboot and held out his hand. "Howdy, Mr. Boot, and welcome to the Cornbread Show."

That's easy! Skidboot placed his paw delicately in the large hand, and they stood momentarily, two males deep into the kind of handshake agreement that had sealed deals throughout Texas history. And since history was only that very minute just rolled away, and history proceeds without ever stopping, it was clear that this minute marked a new kind of history, the first time in Malakoff that a dog had shaken hands for his own $500 contract.

"Well now, the dog and I agreed on the show today." He stood back, balancing on his Tony Lamas that bit the dust with wedged leather points. An overdressed man for the occasion, everyone thought.

"This dog seems to have a high level of cognitive reasoning.!"

David was quick. "No sir, he's been to the vet and had all his shots. He don't have anything *like* that."

They laughed, easy and companionable, everyone getting more comfortable with the idea of performance. David had swallowed his discontent and gritty sense of embarrassment, deciding just to go with events and see what happened. It was a sunny day, clear as glass, a day without horseflies, some might say. Why not take advantage of it?

"We'll have a booth set up for you, probably over there under the trees." Reese gestured at a line of drooping oaks that spattered shade on the fuming ground. The dark line looked inviting. Maybe people would stroll over there just to avoid the sun.

"Now, this place fills up fast. They come for cornbread and lemonade but they stay for the fun. And when I see a crowd out there enjoyin' your dog, then I'll know that Skidboot here is a real show dog."

Reese reached down again toward Skidboot, who stared at him. *What now?*

Russell whispered, "shake hands, Skidboot!"

Skidboot reached his paw delicately up toward Mr. Reese, who failed to understand the gesture at first. Skidboot tapped him on the thigh, once. Reese stared down, looked surprised, and stuck out his hand. Again, they shook.

David felt a flash of something. Not exactly anger, but a feeling of being secondary to a Blue Heeler dog that seemed capable of making his own arrangements.

"And the money?" Now he could get tough.

"Well, when I see that crowd, son, then you get your $500. You know this is pro-ba-tionary to start with."

David nodded. *Wasn't everything?* He understood that a small venue like the Cornbread Festival had low expectations, and the crowds would be mesmerized by anything different, even if a dog just barked out "hello" or rolled on command. Lucky for him, their booth was at the perimeter, which meant that maybe, just maybe, Randy and company might stay toward the center and not stroll out to the edge.

Still, as he watched the cocky cowboy strutting closer, David felt a surge of anger.

"We're going," he urged Russell. "This is *not* going to happen. Russell sized the situation up immediately and instinctively threw a stick into Coyle's path. The stick sailed in the air and landed with a plop. David swiveled around, Skidboot quivered. They both looked at Russell, who looked impassively back. Like magic, the dog flashed through the air and landed in front of Coyle, in front of the stick.

"Stop right there." David's voice was low, authoritative as he purred through the rest of the commands, "ease up on it," " a little more," " raise your left hand," "raise your right hand," "turn this way," "turn that way." Skidboot slid through the commands, ignoring the crowds that gathered around, ignoring the red-faced Coyle.

Skidboot delicately touched the stick, a touch as light as a moth. Coyle spat on the ground, jostled his friends, complained loudly that *any dog can play fetch.*

"Can any dog do this?"

David instructed Skidboot to pick up the trash. Why, he said, there was so much trash around, ice cream cone remains, hot dog wrappers, newspapers and such that Skidboot should do his civic duty and help out. "Go ahead," he urged the dog, "go and pick up all the trash and put it in the trash bin."

David shook inside. He'd given Skidboot a fresh new order, one never voiced before, and even though they had played versions of it, he had no idea if Skidboot would understand or not. David sweated as Skidboot stared at him, so intently he thought they'd both fall over from staring. Then Skidboot calmly trotted over to a dented coke can crushed beneath a wire fence, picked it up by its tab, lifted himself up to the trash bin and dropped it in.

The crowd gasped.

Skidboot found a corn cob, a mangle of deflated balloons and a candy wrapper squeezed flat with chocolate. Solemn as a surgeon, he daintily nipped the trash items, transported them and disposed of them. People clapped, Coyle frowned, and David marveled at how this dog managed to pick up cues, or recognize words, or read his expression, or even understand his words. How? He didn't know. But dawning on him every day was the knowledge that God, in His heaven, had sent David something very, very special to liven things up.

But every blessing has its drawbacks, which David discovered when someone asked the unfortunate question. One that children have always asked of dogs, one that called for the most obvious dog-trick scenario which, for some reason, they'd never rehearsed. "Mama, can the dog play dead?"

"Play dead!" Voices chimed, people catching the notion. Of all the tricks, this one was so obvious!

Dead? David thought.

Skidboot hitched up one ear and gazed up under his brows. *Dead?*

The moment dragged on, voices clamoring. David repeated the command, an unfamiliar one, one that he wished he could interpret in some kind of dog shorthand, something that Skidboot would pick up. After all, he'd learned the trash trick...David thought he might throw himself down on the ground and show him how, but that wasn't part of the plan. Skidboot looked genuinely confused. David had never seen this dog confused before.

Kids complained, adults muttered. Gradually, the crowd drifted away, and David pulled his hat was so far down low on his head, trying not to watch. His hat was so far down he didn't see the man approach him, stand still, blocking the sun, until finally his shadow announced him. And when David looked up, the man coughed gently, then said, "Howdy there, aren't you David Hartwig?" And when David nodded, he recollected that time that David had won the calf-roping championship, described in such glowing terms that David cheered up.

"So, you laid up a while?" David nodded. Yes, obviously.

Gus nodded sympathetically. He was scouting talent acts for the State Fair rodeo talent contest, offering a thousand dollars to the winner. David looked surprised, pointed to his leg, said he wouldn't be riding any time soon.

Gus looked surprised, then pointed to Skidboot. "I'm thinking about the dog, actually. We're always on the lookout for animal talent." Then, as an afterthought, he said kindly, "Of course, that's until *you* get back in the saddle."

He handed David his card, tipped his hat and walked away.

"A thousand dollars!" Russell was practically dancing, one boot to the other.

David mused about the *easiness* of this so called thousand dollars. He considered how long he'd have to shoe horses to earn a thousand dollars, doing hard work he never regretted, work that strained his muscles and taxed his patience and had to be completed before earning a penny. He had to eye the horse first, see if it walked level. Any misalignment meant he had to trim to even it up. He'd take off the dead sole, trim the wall back, shape the shoe right up to the white line of the foot. That's where the nails go, right into the white line. Then he'd clip off the nails that protruded out. David never regretted farrier work, which was an honest, hard enterprise. The good news was that a horse's feet grow a half-inch every thirty days, which meant that most saddle horses needed their shoes reset every three to six weeks. A man's work. Unlike this carnival business of telling a dog to fetch and *winning money from it.*

David sighed. *Worse things could happen*, he guessed.

CHAPTER TWENTY-ONE

Play Dead, *Now!*

Barbara was up early, bringing coffee to David, curious about the day's events. She'd come home too late to hear the story.

"How'd it go?"

Both looked at her, David with a long face, Russell excited. "Mom, someone offered Skidboot a *thousand dollars* just for doing tricks!"

"Is that so?" She eyed David, thinking that this was good news. Why the long face?

Then he told her about the humiliation, the crowd that had gathered, the $500 *not* given because the dog didn't know how to *play dead.* She slowly stirred her coffee, adding just a dab of milk, watching the dark liquid swirl around. She needed to point something out to him, something peculiar.

"Like that?" She gestured to the floor just as Skidboot teetered over, stiff legged, and fell to the ground.

"What the...?" David's first thought was *poison* that some neighbor had had enough of his chicken killing, peacock chasing and calf rustling to take revenge. His next thought was, *the dog did it!*

Skidboot lay rigid on the ground, paws clawed outward in a final rigor, eyes staring straight ahead. Barbara giggled, Russell laughed, and David, flustered, yelled at Skidboot to get up.

The dog contracted all its stiff, dead parts and sprang to his feet, quivering and alert.

"Play dead!" David instructed, wondering if he was crazy or the dog was.

Skidboot fell like a stack of firewood, feet straight out, eyes glazed. He made no effort to break his fall, just landed with a "thud" on the trailer floor, obviously doornail dead.

"Skidboot, get up!" Again, like a released arrow, he shot to his feet and pointed his nose to the sky, one ear cocked, with that same unfathomable, bright gaze that looked slightly deranged, but was, David had come to see, a kind of pleading, as in *ask me something, ask me anything, let's just do it!*

David and Russell spent the next half hour trying to figure out who had cued Skidboot on dead dog behavior, and the best they could figure was that it had been part of their conversation, using "dead" over and over. But how would Skidboot know what "dead" looked like? Had Russell shown him? Throwing himself to the ground, playing possum? Russell shook his head, "no," maybe David had? David firmly denied it, being on crutches and not inclined to horseplay. Barbara, equally puzzled, recalled Skidboot watching that episode of Hawaii 5-O, the one with the shootout. They scratched heads, speculated, agreed that if it were the shootout scene, then Skidboot would be listening for gunfire, not the words "play dead."

Like dealing with a person, David thought, and it began to sink in, ever so slowly, that he was looking at a will to succeed about as powerful as his own. This dog was trying so hard to tune into David that he'd spun the dial past dog, clear into some other realm. And just as David poured affection and wisdom and teaching moments into his stepson, Russell, he now had another responsibility wagging itself silly in the corner, one he might be able to satisfy with a milk bone or a toy, but not really. That dog was relentless. Life, David noted, is full of surprises. One of which arrived the next day.

Barbara, looking through the mail, saw it first. She put down her cup of coffee and failed to pick it back up again. She noted that the clock, stuck on 2:35 pm, needed a battery. Seeing the slight rust blooming up the side of the refrigerator, the unswept area along the shelf that she'd missed, so many things to keep track of, she didn't want Russell within earshot; it made no sense to upset the boy. She brought the foreclosure notice over to David.

> *You have fallen behind in your mortgage payments. If you do not bring your loan current within 30 days of the date of this letter we will start legal action which may result in the foreclosure of the property.*

Her sigh rustled with resignation. It chilled him; he felt her trying to catch her breath. On instinct, he crumpled the letter, then thought better of it and unwadded it. David and Barbara looked long and hard at each other, factoring their life's events, trying to gauge, out of these new circumstances, *how serious.*

"What now, David?"

"I don't know, but I'll think of something."

CHAPTER TWENTY-TWO

The Breakthrough

So far, Skidboot's training had been haphazard, something David pursued part-time and mostly to avoid any repeat of the dead chickens. He wanted to teach Skidboot manners, that was all. But one afternoon he read something that changed this approach, in fact, changed his mind completely about Heeler dogs, his dog, and the relationship of man to beast–forever. The article turned up in *Farm Life* and described the difference between two types of dogs, headers and heelers.

Headers were fetching dogs, the ones used to keep livestock milling around in a group. A header shot to the front of the herd to nip and bark at the animals, forcing them to congregate, to turn right, turn left, buck, dart or stop. Headers were whip smart, highly trainable, and could practically run a herd alone. Wolf-like, the header would circle, nip, pounce, prod the cattle, boss of a dusty herd that he kept between himself and the cowboy.

Heelers, on the other hand, were just as headstrong, in fact, they had no "quit" at all. Once embarked, it was hell to distract them or change their minds. But they operated differently. Instead of coming at the animals from the front and working them toward the cowboy, they worked from the back of the herd, driving them from behind toward the rider.

Now that's interesting. David idly tossed a milk bone to Skidboot, who streaked across the floor, skidded to a stop and buried his snout in the treat. David watched him, then tossed another bone. Just as Skidboot started after it, David moved in behind the dog and closed his big hands over the dog's haunches. Like flood water over a dam, Skidboot surged ahead, yet David held him back.

Skidboot, frantic, turned to nip David's hands.

Each time, David said "whoa," then loosened his grip.

Skidboot buckled nearly into a ball, then shot forward, trying to escape, but David gripped his sleek back into lockdown, hissing, "Whoa!"

Three times it happened: "Whoa" then the hard grip. "Whoa," then the grip again. By the third release, Skidboot paused, and in that instant, David said, "go get it," and Skidboot streaked toward the biscuit. Midway, David calmly repeated, "Whoa." Unbelieving, Skidboot stopped dead still, inches from the milk bone, trembling.

"Go get it." Skidboot snapped up the treat, too excited to eat, knowing this was more about power than food, more about learning than just chasing chickens.

David, equally excited, marveled at what he'd uncovered. He'd been *behind* the dog, not in front. Heelers worked from behind, and he'd worked with the dog's own oddball global positioning system. He'd have to tell the rest of the family that if anyone wanted to tell

Skidboot to "sit" they should make sure *to do it from behind*. The same for "lay down" or anything else they could think of. As time went on, they began to substitute treats, then one day a stick, which the dog gnawed, flailed with and chewed to an arrow shaft. The next, a biscuit that disappeared without even a gulp. But the foremost treat, the item Skidboot seemed to treasure above all was a stuffed animal. Although "treasure" for Skidboot meant snarling at the toy, ripping it to shreds, then shredding the shreds while tossing his head around and growling deep in his throat, snarling like a trapped beaver and generally making such a dust-up that they had to go outside under the shading oak tree.

What a day! Sunny, with the usual clouds converging to the West, thunderheads like freighters colliding on the horizon, then sinking down below the skyline. Jerking himself out of the reverie, David had a fence to mend and made sure that the wire clippers and fencing pliers were packed in with his supplies. Fence mending, metaphors aside, was a skill as old as private property, and in Texas, had been the job of the old-time cowboys who would "work the line" for weeks, never coming back to the ranch house, surviving harsh winters rolled in a bedroll, gulping inky cowboy coffee — mostly grinds — while patrolling hundreds of miles of barbed wire. Since sheep men, Indians and others, too, hated the fences, seeing them as a way to collect fierce tumbleweeds and strangers' livestock, everyone tried to bust through them. The lone rider's job was to maintain the fence, no matter how isolated, freezing cold, lonely or hungry a job it seemed

"Skidboot, let's go to work!"

David knew that he was a hard worker, a man whose mind snapped down around some impossibility like a bear trap. And once locked on, he turned relentless. Nothing could get him off. He guessed if he'd been a dog, it might be a pit bull. It was with this same snarling determination that man and dog faced each other that August day. Both bright-eyed and stubborn, one bound to win and the other to cater.

"Get it!" followed by "whoa!" followed by "get it!" and so on, broke the stillness, and after about ten tries, the dog knew to pause within seconds, after which would follow, "get it." David fumed, "sit," then sailed out a biscuit. The dog leaped, a salmon flinging himself skyward, until David stopped him in midair with "whoa!" Skidboot's ears keened for the sound of the command—he *loved* that command! His ears swiveled like radar, spanning after David as he moved.

Finally tired, David told Skidboot, "go play. Go outside, relax!"

Normally, Skidboot would have shot through the opened door, banged the screen and sailed toward the chicken coop, but this time, David held the door open and Skidboot skulked through, eyes pinned on David. Once outside, he sat disconsolately, as he realized that he was a different dog, a dog that aimed to please and as such, was trapped by the wishes and whims of another. And David, instead of the usual terrible impatience when it came to Skidboot, found himself smiling.

"Enough for today!" David finally said. "Go play!!"

What was happening here? A mathematician might identify it as the Babylonians vs. Greek method, in which the Greeks — like professional dog trainers — had general rules of behavior. They based their rules on the Euclidian idea that all theorems could be ordered from simple axioms. Rules were key. You only had to know the rules and you could work from there. The Babylonians, on the other hand — *that is, David* — discarded the rules to work from scratch. They knew all the theories and could apply them if necessary, but by observing, creating from scratch, doing and redoing, they would reach startling conclusions.

David knew that dog training followed time-tested rules, rules that included leash training for 8-weeks, wearing a no-pull harness, choke collar or using in-the-face water spraying. Other puppy socialization was by pretending to be a fellow dog, yelling "ouch" when bitten, to give the puppy a feeling of success. If he thinks he's won over his siblings, he *might* stop biting. Basic obedience was something the Hartwigs had missed during the ideal puppy training time, up to 9-months. By conventional dog training methods, Skidboot was over the hill, past trainability, which made this conversion, this new behavior — alert, vigorous, confident, obedient — so unusual. Most dog trainers would need from 6-9 months of committed procedures, from fetch and tug of war, to voice training, to even begin to see results. They would train for hours, repeating commands over and over.

"I try a trick once or twice," David said, "and if Skidboot doesn't pick it up, and I mean *right away*, then I just drop it." Skidboot's response time defied reason.

Everyone noticed. First Russell, who tried to distract Skidboot with a hug and a milk bone midway during a training session. One youngster teasing another, David understood, and waited until the commotion died down. Russell kept calling the dog, making little smacking noises to indicate *treat, treat,* trying to draw Skidboot's gaze.

But the Blue Heeler, a sphinx of attention, eyes pinned to the future and muzzle pointed skyward, would not be distracted.

"Here Skidboot, Skidboot, Skidboot." Russell bent himself over upside down to make eye contact.

Skidboot ignored him, except for a quick flick of his tail, as in, *later, Russell, I mean it.* This was beneath dignity.

Russell gave up and clomped down the stairs, dragging his jacket and humming. The new intensity around the place felt good, as if something useful and important had dropped into place. Maybe the money problems would go away.

CHAPTER TWENTY-THREE

A Winning Streak

Bulldogging or steer wrestling, taxed David's muscles, pulled them like taffy as he leaned off Hank, galloping around thirty miles per hour, transferring his weight off the horse onto the huge trunk of the steer he was dogging. Bulldogging first hit the rodeo entertainment world when the famous Bill Pickett, a half-black, half-Indian roping wizard who starred in early Wild West shows, invented a technique so farfetched, so laughingly improbable, that it was his alone—no one else dared try it. Pickett would thunder alongside a galloping longhorn steer on Spradley, his always surprised horse, then grab the steer's head and bite its upper lip, which forced the steer to follow his commands. How did Pickett sense this would work? But the idea of "bulldogging" caught on, becoming a favorite rodeo stunt.

David trusted Hank to hold steady as he reached one long arm out to grasp the steer's closest horn, then, like pulling down stars, reached to grasp the far horn to get the leverage to sling himself out of the saddle, to gallop alongside the pounding freight train of the steer. For more time than is safe, the cowboy stretches out between the steer and his horse, hanging like laundry, his feet somehow still in the stirrups. Before inevitable death, he lets the horse carry him so close to the heaving steer that, with a huge thrust, he jerks his feet from the stirrups and slides along the ground, dirt flying as he tries to brake the steer's speed. He twists its head, but meeting resistance, he throws his weight backwards, slamming the steer into a high speed halt. As the steer spins out, he thunders to the ground.

He'd first gotten into steer wrestling despite his timidity, his low position of last out of seventy doggers and his lack of even a personal horse. He'd scoped out the cowboys who owned bulldogging horses, extraordinary steeds, basically race horses so elite they were beyond most budgets. Not unlike the historic cowboys of the old west, who were often so broke they only had a saddle and had to borrow the ranch horse in order to work. Bulldogging riders might occasionally loan out their horses as long as the recipient could ride.

"Ask old Harold Davidson," they told David. "He'll let you."

When David asked for a loan of the horse, Davidson hardly took the time to consider, just said, "Yes! If you can get your ass out of the box, then go ride!" David shot to the top of the chart in one competition, and after this, his bulldogging success commenced.

Lately, David had raked in prizes for bull wrestling as well as roping, and now, with Skidboot trotting along behind him, was attracting so much attention it felt, well, *blessed.* A new excitement chased through him. Like the faithful at Lourdes, he'd thrown off his crutches and found traction; he was up, riding, and ready for success.

When those little Holstein calves shot out, he was ready with neck rope, two piggin' strings, a horn knot, his knife, and his ankle brace. He knew how to flank and how to coax his horse like his own shadow to follow his every move. He felt confident about catching them and *did*. He knew how to get off, how to flank, and he knew his horse, like his own shadow, followed his every move.

Not only was he sizzling at calf roping but at bulldogging too, when exceeding at two events was nearly impossible for a so-called *mature* rider. Most riders were so young they even failed at shaving. Yet here he was, late-thirties, his balance off, his bones aching, joints on fire, fingers and wrists sprained and strained but on a winning streak that was *bigger than Dallas* with his dog right there at his side. In fact, riding shotgun!

His buddies noticed both his steady winning streak and his dog. They saw him pull up at the Majestic 12 Theater, or the Local Harvest grocery store, or the gas station, Skidboot's muzzle practically pasted to the front window, his eyes glazed with excitement. The dog sensed a rodeo long before they got there and trembled with excitement.

They noticed Skidboot when David was saddling Hank by the trailer, and when they passed, David would tell Skidboot to fetch a stick. They'd stop to watch and see Skidboot do his "stop and start" routine. "Hold it," David would say and Skidboot would freeze. "Back up," he'd say, and the cowboys standing around were so enthralled that a few would make an involuntary backwards step, then laugh with embarrassment. To prolong the drama, David informed Skidboot, very seriously, that yes, he could have the stick but *first,* he had to run around the red truck, or turn left at the hot dog stand, or corner right by the balloons and then come back.

People murmured, then clapped and yelled. People brought so many friends that every time David pulled up, there'd be more pinched front cowboy hats, bobbing like a field of mushrooms, all talking about David and that darn dog. Brodeas Gravvett, a friend of David's, bent over one day and instructed Skidboot to give the stick to the *dumbest man there.* Skidboot, one ear cocked, eyes sparkling, carefully held the stick out to Brodeus. A surge of laughter rang out .

"Show us another!"

"More tricks."

"Hey, does he speak Spanish?"

And so forth.

Last year, Gus had asked him about the Texas State Fair, even offered him $1,000 in prize money. David wondered where the days had gone, his life had whipped around so fast with the riding, the prizes, the success, as well as the daily drilling of Skidboot. He was a different dog by now, with an intuitive sense that almost preceded the idea. David, no doubt a *dog whisperer,* wouldn't have been surprised to find that Skidboot whispered back, so neatly did their thoughts mesh.

"Barbara, I've been thinking. I didn't like the whole performance idea before, you know, that whole *cornbread deal.*" It actually pained him to think of that particular embarrassment. She nodded, she understood.

"But we still got bills, and we still got Skidboot. I'm thinking I might go after that State Fair money."

Barbara nodded, wondering whether David could stand to share the glory with their dog. Her husband was a born champion, someone who climbed after wins the way spiders walked their own webs. It was born in him, and now, he'd be giving part of it away. She shrugged. They both knew that times were changing, that fate was having its way with their lives.

CHAPTER TWENTY-FOUR

Finding the Phone

David lay flat on the grass. Skidboot lay flat on the grass, or as flat as his tightly wound self allowed him. They stared at each other, face to face. No reason, actually. Except David was trying to fathom how far he could trust Skidboot. The Bonham, Texas, rodeo producers had called him up yesterday, something that, in the old days, would have made him stagger with excitement. Only now, they weren't calling about his calf roping. They were calling about his dog.

The Bonham rodeo was a once-a-year family rodeo held on a private ranch. He'd tried to get entry there a couple of times, but the owner, Haynes Cochran, a locally recognized tightwad, had hemmed and hawed, allowing that David might strut his dog across the track a few times, but he'd really have to wait and see. Meanwhile, David played Skidboot at a Senior Rodeo, a quiet little affair consisting of guys over 40. They'd clapped politely, grew quiet and waited to be entertained.

In the crowd, sat Hayes from the Bohnam rodeo, whose ears rang with the growing applause, and who decided that the dog was amazing after all, and who promptly called David back.

Mr, Hartwig, we've heard good things about this here Skidboot. But we wonder, now, is he ring-worthy? I mean, he's only been out once or twice. Are you confident he's got the grit for the Big Time?

David's response brimmed with so many business words, "responsible" and "arena tried" and "well-trained" that he felt like a Marketing Director of some dot com as he turned his dog into a high tech package. Yet David knew he wasn't any of these things. But he wouldn't share that with the Bonham folks.

David stared at Skidboot, looking deep into indigo pools that snapped with mischief, inquiry, sympathy, challenge and well, friendship. While they held this fixed position, eye to eye, man and beast, he tried to understand how far he could push back against such an animal.

Could he trust Skidboot? A really smart animal, like a really smart person, had imagination, which led to a minefield of extemporization. Why, once Skidboot had followed the "patting" instructions right up to the end, then swiped, hard, like spanking. Once he'd nearly played the piano. Another time, he'd read the traffic light without prompting. Once he'd nearly driven off in the truck. If they were going to make themselves into a show, David needed the confidence to trust Skidboot as much as Hank, his trusted horse. He must be practiced, dependable, yet not too independent, an extension of David himself.

Plus, David knew the truth about his Heeler. Skidboot was not obsessed with trying to *obey* but to prove to David that *David could not trick him!"* The dog loved a challenge. If he could, he would have played chess. But unable to grasp a board or a chess piece, this dog's "game" was just as dire, and he saw David as his worthy opponent. While David tried to check the dog, Skidboot was bent on capture, right up until they changed roles again, one playing trickster with the other.

How could David expect this dog to stay cool when he himself was as edgy as a snake on a razor?

When the phone rang, he nearly whooped to hear, "Mr. Hartwig, you have your price." They would perform at the Bonham rodeo July, 1994—a date that marked the division between amateur and professional. They continued to be on their way.

Incredibly, the phone buzzed the next second and yet *another* rodeo was calling. The Blueridge Rodeo over in Collin County, a small gig, but one willing to take a chance on David. Wes Ward, the genial owner, had heard about them, offered them carte blanche, starting right away. Although a small venue, practice there would be invaluable. It would give him a chance to work Skidboot, to rehearse for the bigger ones to come.

Bonham. Blueridge. Why, that's just the B's, David joked to Barbara, who rolled her eyes and made a protective motion toward Skidboot.

"You just take care of my dog, David," she instructed. Crestfallen, he looked at her. Couldn't she see that the dog was on its way to taking care of them? This was Big Time, and he wanted everyone on board for the fun. Did she think he wasn't treating Skidboot right?

"Barbara, let's do some tricks here in the house." He figured that they could all pitch in, get involved, enjoy the relationship and develop a routine that he could use outside the arena, maybe at the countless churches and schools that were also calling.

The phone shrilled again, and Barbara answered. But David noticed how Skidboot's eyes followed the sound to its source. His ears arched forward like twin radar beacons, twisting toward the moving device.

Any good trainer can pick up cues from the animal, and this one nearly announced itself.

"Russell, you distract him." Russell pitched in, rampaging around the floor with Skidboot while David hid the phone under a pile of cushions.

"Barbara, you call the house number with your mobile." An instant later, the phone rang.

Without any rehearsal, David said, "go find the phone."

Skidboot swiveled in place, nose like an arrow. This, without rehearsal! He somehow got the command, understood "phone" at the end of the familiar "go get," and trotted over to the pillows, rummaged through and found the landline. He pawed it once as in—*there it is folks, anything else?*—and turned for approval. For a Blue Heeler, bred to run herds into the horizon, to nip at hooves, direct a phalanx of outsized cattle toward a pinpoint destination, the mere unearthing of a shrilling piece of plastic probably seemed...elementary.

"That's fan-tas-tic!" Skidboot, eyes narrowed, watched everyone cavort around, excited, trying to come up with another task. If only they understood the wild strain that ran through him, the echoes of open plains, vast canyons, the daily need to eat or be eaten, so primal that no humans, at least not these humans, could ever understand. Skidboot himself didn't understand, because this instinct slipped into his cortex from the primal brain, and lodged there, forcing him to find prey, *no matter how ridiculous.*

To Skidboot's delight, they decided on another piece of *prey*, the tiny black-hand device that turned the talking box on and off, called, appropriately, The Remote! He obligingly left the room while they "hid" it. Unlike the wild veldt of Australia, where every burrow or hole must be explored, where a red rock crevice might house a family of dusky hopping mice or a burrowing Betong, where sand hills sheltered long-tailed Dunnarts and spotted Chudditch, the Hartwig living room had only about three possible hiding places. He sighed.

David slipped the remote under the sofa cushion, then Russell sat down on the sofa.

"Skidboot!" David commanded. "I want to watch television." A complex thought using words that he didn't think would register, without rehearsal, but then, he was not thinking in the same primal way. Skidboot calmly, methodically, began to eliminate possibilities. You could almost see him keeping a list, *not here, not under the sofa, not under the cushion, not behind the ficus.* Then he stuffed his sharp nose under a pile of ironed shirts and delicately prized it out.

David was so startled he nearly spilled his coffee. The only thing he could think now was if such quick discovery looked too practiced. How could he get Skidboot to nose around in the wrong places, or maybe, drag it out a little? No one would believe that he could just trot directly, so quickly, over to the device.

"Good dog!" They all jumped up and down, praising Skidboot, excited. Russell carried on as if the dog had made a touchdown. David hushed them, added a new instruction.

"Skidboot, sir, come here. I want to watch TV, please bring me the remote."

Skidboot mouthed the piece and trotted over to David, happy to do this because both the primal brain and the thinking cortex of the dog understood that there was one being here with more wisdom, strength and ability to dominate than any other wolf, dingo or dog, and that was man. Skidboot had learned this quickly, as had his forbearers.

They looked at each other proudly. *This was incredible.*

Unfortunately, these tricks, good as they were, wouldn't work in a rodeo arena. These were parlor tricks, and they could play indoors at any of the schools, churches or banquets that kept calling. So, David divided Skidboot's talents into two categories: home and arena. His eyes roved around the tiny living room of the Hartwig ranch, saw the shaded mini-lamp, the round tufted area rug, the study alcove where they paid their bills and lighted on the bedroom. Why, any self-respecting dog should learn the basics.

A simple idea, but why not? Skidboot should put himself to bed, and over time, Skidboot's Bed Time captured the hearts of school kids everywhere. When David—just like a father!—towered over his dog and sternly said, "Skidboot, it's time for bed," children understood this finality, and even though they probably wished that Skidboot would rebel, bark out his objections, "no! no!" the way *they* wanted to, Skidboot would grab a pillow and carry it to the middle of the stage. Then, he laid the pillow down and slowly, lowered his head onto it. Hindquarters settled down last, and quite gently, very gradually, he nestled himself into the pillow.

But they weren't through. David then held out a favorite blanket, the thin, almost raggedy blue cotton one, and said, "Skidboot, cover up!"

And Skidboot, to the transfixed children, would grab the blanket in his teeth, tightening himself into a burrito. The kids exploded, laughing, clapping, but even the commotion failed to interrupt Skidboot's sleep. He only "awakened" when David told him—with a "snap" and a "Good boy—to wake up."

Barbara photographed the performances, and they soon had a pile of glossy Skidboot photos for fans. "He's the N-Sync of the dog world," Russell laughed.

"Who?" David and Barbara echoed.

And over time, the number of fans and the number of photos grew, as did the opportunities.

CHAPTER TWENTY-FIVE

Texas State Fair

Skidboot's mouth fell open. He'd seen a lot in a year and a half, but nothing like this. When David called Gus back and said "yes" to the Texas State Fair, it shot them both into a venue of flashing lights, sparkling fountains and a 700-foot long reflecting pool—they'd never seen so much water. Illuminated floats rumbled by, filled with girl scouts and flowers, and overhead, clouds of balloons bobbed like birds. A drum and bugle barrage bellowed away, so loud that Skidboot whined.

"You ok?" David stroked Skidboot, noticed the quivering, but didn't give it much thought. The dog was coiled as a spring, as usual. Maybe it was the effect of seeing his first 15-foot puppet, an outsized head that bobbed and grinned down at them, then fell away as Big Tex, the 500-foot high symbol of the Texas State Fair, loomed overhead. *Big Tex*, David mused, *what a man.*

The fair grew more complicated every year. Once a venue for dairy goat milking parlors, pie contests and 4-H rabbit displays, the fair's agenda now rivaled Disneyland.

About the only familiar thing was the rodeo arena, which brought a brief pang of remorse or nostalgia

"It's always 'Sit,' 'Stay,' 'Heel'—never 'Think,' 'Innovate,' 'Be yourself.'"

PETER STEINER, JUNE 25, 1990

P. Steiner

CHARLES E. MARTIN, JAN. 22, 1972

NEW YORKER COVER PRINTS

Find your favorite cover
on virtually any topic at
NewYorkerStore.com

To order, please visit
NewYorkerStore.co

along with the staccato blare of the loudspeakers. The rage and intensity of the loudspeaker had no scruples; it hammered everyone with its crazed metallic exuberance. People in the stands, maddened by the din, yelled out; he could hear the vocal pitch but not the words. Spotlights glimmered like Hollywood, long beams raking through the night sky. David loved the rodeo at night. He caught a glimpse of a calf roper flying by, just the upper torso, one hand overhead as if in supplication but really, whipping out a lasso that snaked through the night air toward its prey.

CHAPTER TWENTY-SIX

Disobedience

The Hartwigs turned into a celebrity family, *the People With the Dog*, remarked upon wherever they went. At the local diner, Burger & Fries, kids clustered around and begged autographs while David lounged in the red leather booth beneath his own signed photo that hung on the blue wall—David and Skidboot, local celebrities. David couldn't buy a bit at the tack store without strangers sidling up, eager to chat. Apparently, the world loved dogs, and specifically, Skidboot. And the world wanted to know *to the detail* what his next trick would be. David laughed, because really, when he said he didn't know, he was being honest. It irked his pride a bit, but when it came down to the bucket bottom, the tricks were mostly up to Skidboot. He hated to admit this, because the idea of being in charge motivated him through this weird and constantly unfolding adventure, but it was more hope than reality. The dog, like some furry little Benjamin Franklin, constantly tested the limits of invention, always veering off into a surprising new direction, like that time he refused to eat his treats until David read off the ingredients.

But any publicity was good publicity, and as success lapped around them, their boat lifted high over the usual flotsam of debt, disorder and doubt. David's confidence, always high, nearly lifted his hat, and the surge of energy drew Barbara's affections ever more in his direction. Mornings, now, she brought him fresh brewed coffee in bed, before she left to work. And smiling, too. As folks with momentum, they ate occasional steak for breakfast and bulged their bank account at every ring of the phone. Once their lives felt simple, if impoverished. But today, their own investment portfolio frolicked happily in the living room. It fetched, rolled over and brought home piles of cash.

Daily, the phone shrilled like a bird, hopping off its landline hook with queries from promoters, league directors, church organizers, festival planners and rodeo associations seeking Skidboot's talents. Most of them knew David, respected him, remembered him from the world of calf roping. They trusted him to put on a good show.

Skidboot had been at it now for more than two years, performing with laser sharpness. The pair—David and Skidboot—would lope into the arena like Siegfried & Roy, practiced, casual, yet both with defined goals. David's main goal was to *withhold* what Skidboot wanted, panted after, snarled for and unwaveringly fixed his desires upon—the toy. Skidboot was fixed on trying to outwit David and get the toy, even as David, by turning into an ogre of negativity and steel, would force Skidboot to stop in his tracks, reverse himself, shake hands, turn in circles, pirouette like a dancer, and otherwise execute his litany of dazzling maneuvers, doing *anything* to get the prey. For David, the prey meant pay. For Skidboot, the prey meant the toy. On Wall Street, they would call it free market capitalism. In Quinlan, Texas, it was a flat out miracle.

Miracle, indeed. So they all believed as the lucky, looping feedback system from man to dog and back to man spun out until David wondered, sometimes, if he was in his right mind. An optimist would think, *it's what we've always deserved!* A realist would say, *I'm scared, what next?*

The next day, as if in response to his own thoughts, David felt a chill of apprehension. Something was off. He'd spent too long with this dog, knew him too well, and, like seeing a pig at a pay phone, sensed something offbeat.

Nothing seemed amiss at first. The blare of the horn, dust rising up as the last bull rider flew in the air, hat sailing, and also signaling half time, when the dog and man show would perform. Skidboot seemed calm, no skittishness at the size of the crowd, the noise, the applause as he trotted into the arena, back bristling, nose sharp, reminding everyone of Blue Heeler aggressive superiority, that like his kind, he was a dog so dominant he'd die before quitting. He ruled, and he let them know it. The crowds instantly recognized his bristling authority, and it was what they wanted. Working folks *wanted* a dog that taunted and tasked his master because it struck one good blow for the underclass, who felt a lot like the dog most of the time. But then, for drama's sake, they also wanted the *dog* to give in and comply with the master, who after all was a cowboy — like them — and particularly deserved respect and power. Arena psychology, David thought. *Deep.*

Skidboot stopped and sat, scanning the crowd. David sauntered after, a tall man in Levi's and hat, his soothing voice belying generations of steely resolve. People who knew Hartwig called him *that stubborn German*, a man who never took anyone else's word for anything unless he'd proven it out himself. Yet he struck folks as oddly sentimental, too. No one could figure it out.

David stilled the dog, his Texas twang low, insinuating, spinning a soothing aural effect.

"Ok, now just wait right there until I count to three."

Skidboot threw him a glance. David felt uneasy.

"One" Skidboot eyed the toy.

"Two." Skidboot began to tremble.

David sped through his numbers but before his eyes, *long before he slipped in the number three* — Skidboot took off and grabbed the toy!

He'd shortstopped David, who hung there, dumbfounded while mouthing "seven."

The crowd roared with laughter. Skidboot gnawed at the toy, daring David to bully him, discipline him, show his master chops in public. Trying to capture the moment and ride the new momentum, David turned the tables, announcing *now there's a dog that wants to be in charge. This dog can darn well improvise!* The crowd loved it, hooted, yelled "Skidboot, Skidboot!" *Hilarious*, they thought.

But not David. As they drilled through a few more tricks, he watched Skidboot strut like a little peacock, knowing that David couldn't punish him here in front of all these people. And every time, Skidboot anticipated the magic number and broke the drill, bolting forward on some number of his own choosing, his eyes alight, tail trembling with the fun of it. Now the tables were turned. He had David under his control!

Fuming, sweat beading under his hat, David finished the routine through gritted teeth. *You are gonna catch it, Skidboot,* he mouthed, and as soon as they'd cut through the gate and were behind the fence, he bellowed. But he also realized that it was too late, this miscreant behavior had to be nipped when it happened, not later. A chill shuddered up him, looking at the dog. It was like seeing a familiar friend suddenly transformed by madness, or by slit-eyed dementia, or even by strange, grisly hatred. He studied the dog, seeing the familiar spots, the whorls of fur along his nose, the arched doggie brow—so familiar—yet Skidboot, unbelievably, had become a different animal. Skidboot had gone arena sour.

"Arena sour? What's that?" Both Barbara and Russell frowned, puzzled. Russell's cheeks flushed and Barbara's lustrous eyes squinted. Pondering the new development, they sipped ice tea around the table, clustered in a family meeting. Spoons clinked, sugar swirled, but no one reached for the cookies, no one even bothered to drink once they'd heard the prognosis. Their dog had inexplicably and undeniably turned rogue. Their *Skidboot!* But the evidence lingered, visible to everyone. They'd seen Skidboot prancing around to his own drummer, disobeying David, setting the crowds nearly hysterical when they realized the dog was flaunting the master.

"Arena sour is what happens to horses when they know you can't discipline them. In public, they *know* you can't take out the whip and whack them, or lash them with a piggin' string. It's *street smarts*, horse style. They know the crowd protects them."

They all turned to stare at Skidboot. *Arena sour? Spoiled dog? Like some over-coddled movie star?* For a brief second, they had a glimpse of the usually shrouded canine mind, intelligent, devious, able to be *man's best friend,* to have his back, but just as quickly, to revert back into the primal past, using its manlike decision skills to even the score.

Skidboot, now so manipulative, so duplicitous, as to seem *almost human,* behaved exactly like a 9-year-old, yet with adult wisdom. Shockingly calculating behavior for man's best friend, but predictable, since the canine brain circuit responds to rewards, and Skidboot, now primed to David's authoritarian regime, viewed the public respite of the arena—a place that he knew he could escape from David's demands in the same way he might respond to food—a reward. He had a clear, visual signal, the safety of the crowd. Doggy dopamine released, flowed, filling him with the neurohormones of happy anticipation. A successful feedback loop—applause, then rewards.

"Naw, I've seen it in horses. It's not unusual," David's reassurances felt empty, he really wasn't sure how this would go. Yet oddly enough, the crowds loved it. The performance was better than ever.

Everyone, apparently, loved an underdog, even if it was a man.

Everyone loved that Skidboot turned the tables. Whether rehearsed or spontaneous, they only knew it worked.

But not for David. "Skidboot," he hissed, and Skidboot, as if struck by a snake, stood waiting.

"Dog, you are taking advantage."

Skidboot cocked an ear, looked up at the smiling, laughing faces, at hundreds of human faces, laughing at him, having fun, and he felt a surge of pride. *Yes..so?*

David gripped his piggin' string, fighting back the idea of punishment that welled up. Teeth gritted, he strode around in front of Skidboot and kneed him toward the exit, pushing his blue butt outside even as Skidboot, crowd crazy, dug in and longed back toward the bleachers, his tail beating and his muscles, ropy and strong, fighting to keep from being hustled out.

"You are gonna learn, dog, if it takes a lifetime!" They stared at each other. Then Skidboot relaxed, gave a shake of his tail, waved his paw at the bleachers and pranced out.

David was astonished. *Waving goodbye...? What next?*

CHAPTER TWENTY-SEVEN

Losing Control

David felt crushed. All those months of training, the split-second responses, the careful backing forward, backwards, sideways, on demand. Now the dog was rogue, adding his own version of behavior. It offended David, even though the crowds loved it.

"We're never gonna get called back," he told Barbara, looking at the water bill, and that electricity bill, hadn't they paid it?

But the rodeos kept calling. Seems that the same people who loved to see the dog obey also loved to see him *disobey*, and David, hardworking, earnest, and abiding, couldn't disguise his reaction to the dog's disobedience. Despite his efforts to relax, to go with Skidboot's flow, to cover up each breach, everyone knew the instant that Skidboot went maverick, and would roar with approval.

"Why not just go with it, David?"

"It's funny!"

"They love it."

Angry, his mind racing, David refused. "No way! The crowds are giving him the reward, and the dog is training himself. That will not fly, not here, not with me. *Why, would you let Russell train himself?* He couldn't think of a perfect analogy, but he knew it was in there somewhere. *You just didn't let dogs or children train themselves!*

The program was falling apart. The dog was turning the tables, and *damn* if David wasn't the dog and Skidboot the master. From then on, nearly every rodeo appearance spiked with a flippant show of disobedience, one that David couldn't punish on the spot because of the onlookers, one that he couldn't punish *afterward* because it was *too late*. Sometimes Skidboot would execute a trick with flawless obedience, just like the old days, but other times, he'd gaze up at the crowds, lift his eyebrow, and when he had everyone full of suspense, lavishly disobey the commands. David, more and more angry, was having a hard time playing second man to a Blue Heeler.

CHAPTER TWENTY-EIGHT

The Animal Psychic

One night, Barbara chatted quietly on the phone, looking up at David occasionally, shaking her head, then continuing. He watched her, wondering about the conversation.

"David," she said softly after, "I have an idea." He listened as she described a friend's success story with an unruly dog, how her friend, at wit's end, had called in a kind of an animal *therapist*. Now he'd heard everything.

Therapist? What kind of a therapist?" Why, even if they needed one themselves—which he'd thought possible at times—he'd never go to one. Expensive, invasive, useless. No way.

"It's an animal psychic, David."

"Psychic?" He guffawed, pulling his hat off and sailing it across the room. "Look, a space ship!" Barbara stiffened. She was just *suggesting*, after all. Psychics, close kin to palm readers and numerologists, had discovered the animal world, along with the pet owners willing to plunk down cash for the emotional health of their beloved pets.

"They commune somehow."

David looked skeptical. "What's next, Barbara? Tarot?"

No one understands it, her friend had told her, but well, the stories! Tales of mental rapport between man and beast usually carried out by people who, from birth, seemed different, yet were sensitive to the animal mind and able to interpret a pet's cloudbuzz of unarticulated query, musings, inquiry, dislikes, yearnings and mulish irritations. Did they only read dogs, David wondered? Or could they pick up the mind waves of cats, low-flying birds, ferrets? Why, for a person like this, a walk in the park must turn into sensory pachinko. Information overload.

"We could at least try it, "Barbara stiffened. David always had to be so *right*.

After a day or so, he relented. What harm, might as well, it'd be something to laugh about later, except for the expense. Plus, he couldn't tell any of his friends. This psychic deal had to be secret, but to make Barbara happy, they'd do it quickly and get it over with.

Barbara promised to handle the details and Russell swore himself to silence, while David mused on life, authority, effectiveness, unregulated industries — like pet whispering — and his own ambitions, now brought to a strange pass by this loopy interaction. He worried that just the idea of it might interfere with Skidboot's reputation. He rejected any notion of dream interpretation or chatting with the spirits of the animal dead. Yet here they were, skirting around the paranormal with a dog that was, well, he had to admit it, a little paranormal himself. David, as well as most of science, knew that language was human specific. How was it possible to interpret a dog's mind, translate it into words, and then spin it back into conversation with the dog? If anyone could read *his* mind they'd hear *just hurry and get this over with.*

The day of the psychic interview began like any other. Soft morning breezes blowing, dewy and glistening. A Texas morning summoned up longing in a body, the memories of better times, the tender turn of the sun before it turned into a blister of heat. Mornings were gentle respites before the sun's fury kicked in.

They arrived at her house, a recessed two-plex, nondescript, to greet the psychic. Mrs. Ada Bellon, whose focus blew past them and fixed completely on Skidboot. She probed the dog, starting out gently: "What are you thinking about when you see all the people?" "Do you really intend to disobey?" "Are you just helping David, or do you want to do harm?" "No? Then what are your intentions?" "Are you upset about anything?" The questions, as far as David could tell, netted about zero. Skidboot responded the way David felt that he himself might respond, with puzzled looks and a cocked ear, looking around for clues, but adrift. Maybe Skidboot needed an incentive — a toy — or maybe better yet, David thought briefly, he needed coaxing with the piggin' string!

David mentioned this. Mrs. Bellon then "asked" Skidboot what he thought about the piggin' string. Skidboot *might* have had an opinion, probably *did* have an opinion, but wouldn't say. Nothing seemed to interest him. He stared at the flocked walls, the overstuffed sofa, the slow-ticking clock. Without a toy to fix on, or a command to puzzle over or even subvert, without snacks, without a clapping crowd chanting his name, or a clown cavorting around the arena, Skidboot felt boredom crawl over him. *Doesn't she already know? What difference does it make?*

Politely, he just stared at her.

Finally, the hour was over, a stretch of time that lasted far longer than normal for everyone, including Mrs. Bellon. She prided herself on her work, an uphill profession on a good day, especially after that failed experiment on Austrian television, where Richard Wiseman designed four psychic dog tests, the chief one being whether the dog knew if his owner was coming home or not. A simple enough request, but the dog publicly failed all four. She knew that her shaky expertise could be explained away as selective memory and multiple guesses, so that she had to work extra hard to eliminate doubts.

But this dog seemed like hard work. He was *resisting*. She consulted her notes, paused, said that she understood that Skidboot had issues. Issues, she pointed out, usually took a while to clear up. She would be happy to work with them all, perhaps weekly?

Seeing David's reaction, she hurried up with the news that Skidboot resented authority and probably missed his puppyhood, having been yanked out of the nest before the others, and this longing could translate into seeking approval from the crowd. Or it also might mean that Skidboot needed time off, more time for nurturing, or at least, for more fun. Even as Barbara nodded, *yes*, David nearly choked on his coffee. *Fun?* He thought. *I'll show you fun.*

CHAPTER TWENTY-NINE

Fake Rodeo Therapy

Every cowboy needs a horse—a dependable horse, one who puts the rider's needs first, has integrity, character and will *have his back*. Every cowboy needs the same thing in a friend, and in Lanham Mangold, David had found it. Lanham was a few years younger than David, a calf roper from Giddings, Texas, a man he'd met roping and liked right away. Mangold seemed like any other of the ropers at first, but time proved out his extreme skills and fine character, as well as a business daring that few arena cowboys demonstrated. Most cowboys were dogged by money issues, failing franchises and busted ranches, while Lanham sailed financially out of the circuit world. A skilled roper, he had shot to the Nationals, which wasn't enough for him. He then started to buy and sell horses and make rodeo deals, eventually forming his own rodeo association, the United States Calf Roping Association, USCRA, a vortex of calf roping and horse sales activity so huge, so dynamic, that it made him a wealthy, successful man.

"Lanham," David called him up one day. "I got a problem."

"Let's hear it."

"My dog's not doing so good." He told him about Skidboot's ornery ringside behavior, how it had ruined their teamwork, and how people, oddly enough, liked their show anyway and wanted him to keep showing the dog, disobedience or not.

"Well, then what's the problem, David? You still got a good gig going."

But the stern girdings of his own nature would not allow David to settle for Skidboot's behavior, popular or not. Especially since that pesky Heeler was inventing more and more bizarre tricks. Whenever it happened, David had to cover up, make it look like he'd really planned it that way.

Lanham squinted at him, struggling not to laugh. David nearly blurted out the psychic story, but caught himself in time. Lanham pushed his hat back. He swung the gate open, then closed, then open again, his eyes bright with interest. This was a *great* story!

"What can I do for you, David? I don't know much about dogs."

David explained his plan, a design so intuitive, so brilliant, and so purely Hartwig, that it seemed foolproof. It was a plan no professional animal trainer would ever concoct, either for reasons of expense or failure of imagination. But David was no ordinary animal trainer. He was intuitive, inventing as he went, and today, he wanted his friend to loan him a rodeo.

You what?

"Just loan me a rodeo, Lanham. Full arena, real people, I'll bring Skidboot, people will be entertained, but I won't charge a nickel. You just have to give me permission to let the audience know that this is a training session, in which certain, well, *strict training procedures* might be publicly applied."

"Like what, David?"

David Hartwig had never shown cruelty to an animal in his life, nor to any living thing. But from Jack London on, any dog owner knew that in the intimacy of a trainer-dog duo not only blossomed love, respect, and a streak of horseplay, but an environment in which the leader proved his Alpha in a high-pitched, teeth first, old school way. If the leader was not The Man, then he would most certainly be the dog. Lately, Skidboot had been slyly pulling the Alpha rug straight out from under David's boots, and David had to snatch it back. Tall and lean, his shadow ran halfway to the bleachers on a sunny day, and with all his height, he figured that the best authority would be a full body throw down flat on top of the dog, then to snarl, growl like a wolf, snap his teeth, tussle with the dog, pinch its ears, restrain its surges and create such a sideshow that the uninitiated might see it as cruelty. But it was never cruel, not ever. David knew this, and he knew that Skidboot knew it, too.

"But will the audience get it?" Lanham frowned, worried about charges of animal abuse, about the tender-hearted cat owners who might see David pummeling and snarling at his dog and call animal services. But he caught the wild brilliance of the plan. With a thousand eyes pinned on Skidboot, his punishment would be public and being so, would force the dog back into a state of obedience.

Once Skidboot saw there was no safety in crowds, he'd get over being arena sour. And if he didn't obey, he'd get pummeled and punished, right on the spot.

"Never heard of such a thing," Lanham mused, although as they chatted, he remembered hearing something similar about horses, how they used the presence of the crowd to go against commands.

"But if you want me to loan you a rodeo, I'll do it just for heck's sake, not to mention friendship. You bet I'll do it."

The event would take place at the Giddings, Texas Circle 2 Arena, a place set up for calf roping and ideal for the public display. On a day like a frying pan, so hot it drove the summer clouds down to cluster along the horizon, too exhausted to fill themselves up and journey skyward, a day of overheated birds and dazed lizards, David and Skidboot strode into the ring. Texas heat seldom interfered with Texas sports and today was no exception.

The bleachers hummed. News was out about the special dog training during intermission, and people were eager to see how it would turn out. Natural perversity and the general, ornery local temperament made it even odds; half were for the dog, half for David.

"Skidboot!" the crowd roared. And David, his smile slightly drooping, placated Skidboot, spoke calmly, and to the audience, pointed out the value of a dog knowing the rules, the dismay he'd felt at this betrayal and how anyone with children could understand the need for discipline. He named the last seven rodeos around the state where Skidboot had

David and Skidboot on Pet Star.

David and Skidboot in the act — Texas State Fair

Skidboot greeted by his younger fans.

David and Skidboot work the crowd.

Skidboot races figure eights around barrels.

Skidboot leads horse by the reins.

Photo taken from top row of arena at State Fair.

David and Skidboot post act with fans.

Skidboot ordering a hot dog to go.

Skidboot takes a break backstage.

'All-American Dog' ad brochure. David and Skidboot
work their magic for the State Fair Of Texas 2001

Backstage before a show.

David and Skidboot prepare for entry to arena.

David and Skidboot enjoy the fans.

More attention from fair goers.

David and Skidboot, front page for 10th Annual Canine Fun Days & Greyhound Reunion

Linda Smith, Errol McKoy and David Hartwig

*Texas State Fair
2001*

Entering the bright lights of the arena.

Skidboot works his tricks a good distance from David.

All done ... and now he listens to me

David and Skidboot after the show.

Skidboot focusing on his master's every command.

More tricks, more fans, more fun.

Posing for a quick photo opportunity.

David converses with event staff.

Another great year at the fair comes to a close.

Skidboot traveling celebrity status.

*David snaps a quick photo of Skidboot photographer
Robert Ritchie and Skidboot.*

Skidboot relaxing in one of his favorite places.

*State Fair of
Texas 2001*

Skidboot, David and Barbara backstage.

David and Skidboot pose for yet another photo.

*Skidboot races figure eights
around barrels.*

Best of friends, best of times.

Skidboot

Skidboot celebrity headshot photo.

Performing for their younger fans.

Skidboot's paw marked in concrete.

deliberately — and here he paused, his disappointment showing — triggered off early or dashed out on the wrong number. Yes, David was taking it personal, and he hoped everyone here would get behind this unusual effort. And many thanks.

A low murmur of approval swelled, or perhaps it was anticipation. David turned to Skidboot to begin the routine.

"You see that toy? I want you to go get that toy. But first, I want you to run over to the clown and touch him. Then run back to me."

Now watch, David clutched with anticipation, as eager for the dog to go wrong as he usually was for Skidboot to obey.

Skidboot delicately paced over to the clown, politely patted his polka dots, then turned and walked back to David, every muscle quivering, his eyes like obsidian.

The crowd clapped, but with murmurs, questions.

"Skidboot, now you go get that toy." The dog took off.

"Now stop." Skidboot stopped.

"Now go very, very slow..." Skidboot snuck up closer.

"Now when I say "three" you *git that toy!*" This was David's capstone moment, when everyone would see Skidboot's hidden ornery nature in this moment of feckless disclosure.

"One,"

"Two,"

"Seven,"

"Fourteen,"

The numbers spun out into boredom, everyone waiting, including Skidboot. *Why isn't that dog breaking out?* It dawned on David that he'd been outwitted, that Skidboot was now on best performance behavior, that Skidboot was not about to get pummeled publicly, that the dog had somehow *understood* what was going on. For a brief second, he wished he had the psychic here, just to get a glimpse of a mongrel mind so convoluted, so facile and so noncompliant.

"Three!" Skidboot dove for the toy exactly on cue, and clamped it firmly in his teeth with a frantic whine of victory. He burrowed his face in the toy, ragged it back and forth, snarling, pacing backwards, flipping his shoulders in a fast-paced, private victory dance. David caught the quick glance Skidboot threw at him. He didn't want to think about it.

The crowd exploded, "Skidboot!" they boomed, the intensity growing, sonic as a slammed door. "Skidboot!" David saw Russell doubled over, laughing, saw Barbara in stitches, and slowly, grudgingly, broke into a smile. It *was* pretty funny. Maybe the psychic was right. All the dog needed was a little fun.

Not even a week later, at the Mesquite rodeo, David launched his special toy trick, the one with the green velour dolphin, one that they'd practiced for over an hour, even though Skidboot looked bored and even though David knew the dog had the details down. Now, as the crowd looked on, David felt the tension, a friable, uncertain thing. Would the dog perform or not?

You bet! Skidboot shot him a glance and with haughty impunity, jumped the gun, pounced on the wrong number, shot David a triumphant look and nosed around to greet the crowd. *Yes, fun!*

They loved it. They knew David wasn't faking, they could see the fumes rising in *real anger*. David grabbed Skidboot, pulled him by the leash quickly across the arena and hauled him behind the chute. It was soon enough between offense and punishment to make a difference, and David shocked whoever could see them by giving out full-force Hartwig discipline. After that, he talked Mangold into letting him "use" another rodeo, which Skidboot also intuited and rigged by performing perfectly. But David had a plan, and no sooner had one promoter called him, than another was on the line. And before long, Skidboot was performing so often that even he got confused — *real rodeo or fake?* — and began to go more and more with David's discipline. Sometimes he forgot, and David was quick to make good on his threats, audience or not. The odds were stacked. Unable to find safety in public places, Skidboot slowly dropped his innovations and settled back into the routine.

"If this dog doesn't get it right, just say 'amen!'"

The crowd stilled, expecting dire results. And with every success, David and Skidboot got more invitations, more performances, and yes, more money. It was all they could do to keep up. Calls every day, major networks wanting interviews. Newspapers concocted new stories, wire services spread the stories, and each story built itself into another story. A flood of publicity carried them along, bringing a new network called PAX and its fledgling show, *Animals Are People Too*. The moderator, Alan Thicke, spun exciting stories about special animals, and after watching a few segments, David was convinced that he'd get a call. The call came, the show happened, and almost effortlessly, David and Skidboot sailed toward stardom.

CHAPTER THIRTY

From Disaster to Jay Leno

Jay Leno didn't know rodeos. He didn't know about trick dogs from Quinlan, Texas, at least not until one of his assistants viewed the PAX special and raved about it. "Jay," he said, "you have to see this dog!" Leno saw the clip and invited them on—not once, but twice, generating rapt audience reaction. Both times proved stressful for David, but in different ways.

The Tonight Show at Studio 11 in Burbank, California, follows an established format, with opening credits, then the announcer, after which comes the first segment, usually a ten-minute monologue by Leno—a potpourri of current event one-liners and brief comedy sketches. The second segment might be a full comedy sketch, or a mini-documentary by a "Tonight Show correspondent." Soon, the first guest appears, the interview divided into two segments. Then comes an interview with the second guest, followed by a musical performance or a brief teaser of stand-up comedy.

For the first time, Barbara would be going along on this venue—the Jay Leno Show!—and the excitement was palpable. Since it was enroute, they scheduled a quick luncheon appearance at the Lion's Club in Sherman, Texas just before catching their flight at

Dallas/Fort Worth airport. The Leno crew had confirmed them in first class, and David couldn't wait to see the three of them eating juicy steaks and sipping champagne. Two Hartwigs and a dog. For the thousandth time, he felt the blessings. It seemed like too much. And, it was.

They'd bought a 1978 camper on wheels, a boxy little 28-foot motor home for future side trips, riding around the countryside, camping, performing at rodeos. But for now, they threw their bags in, slammed the doors shut, and — like a blast from a youthful past — squealed away from Quinlan toward the adventure of their lives. *This will be fun,* Barbara said to David. *Yes, fun,* David replied. They would drive the Sam Rayburn Freeway and turn onto the Buck Owens Freeway, arriving in Sherman with just enough time to perform, to munch wilted chicken strips and pocket the $150 fee, and then roar away to DFW airport.

A typical Texas town, Sherman distinguished itself by once having Jesse James and his outlaw band rampage through town, after which, James was apparently so impressed that he returned to spend part of his honeymoon there. Tornadoes, freight trains and riots have ripped through Sherman, and on Halloween, it's known for a hidden house of horror, tucked away off Taylor Street, next door to a snow cone stand, within sight of Fairview Park and the old Anderson Slaughterhouse. Time and history have left the town just as the Hartwigs found it — a sleepy, uneventful destination, although not for long.

After the performance, with only a few hours until takeoff, David turned the starter and heard an empty "click."

"No way!" He panicked, stomping the pedal, then stopped, afraid of flooding the tank. Again he tried, with the hollow "clicks" sounding like the end of their Los Angeles fantasy, the dying gasp of a broken dream.

David tried to call a cab, but Sherman lay too far north of the airport to have regular taxi routes. Somehow, he and Barbara managed to push the camper—*how? David wondered later, did two humans and a dog shoulder a 4,000-pound camper out of the gas lane?* As they waited for the only cab that responded, David dialed the Leno people. *They are going to cross us off the list.*

But no. Veterans of misfires, screw ups, no shows and missed flights, the Leno coordinator had seen it all before, had dealt with hysterical voices pleading over faraway phones and soothed them with, "don't worry, be happy, we'll get you a new flight, easiest thing in the world..."

They'd stacked a small pyramid of luggage on the ground, and when David gave the ignition a final, angry twist, and the engine shockingly purred to life, they had to fling the bags back into the camper, Barbara desperately trying to shove them in while David shouted, "let's go, let's go!" then peeling away while Barbara struggled to secure the door. Luggage dropped around them like ripe fruit. Skidboot pasted himself to the front window with his usual bombardier focus, ears perked, stiff-legged with the careening momentum of the camper, as if flying a Spitfire mission.

David and Barbara yelled, argued, and pleaded with each other while dodging a flying phalanx of airborne work gloves, *Texas Monthly* magazines and a scatter of empty water bottles. A cabinet door sprang open, ejecting tuna cans, sponges, dog food and cleaning cloths, turning the camper into a comic road version of the sorcerer's apprentice, everything hellishly animated and airborne.

They squealed into long-term parking, the camper nearly upending as they torqued to a stop. David, horrified, realized that he'd driven to a place so distant from the terminal that he'd never be able to limp fast enough to cover the distance, two-miles away. The sky winked at them, as if this was the funniest thing to have come along all day.

"We need a shuttle bus!" They spotted one a few turnouts away, its yellow roof jaunty and inviting, and grabbing, dragging, limping and perspiring, they flagged it down. With relief, David and Barbara moved to board when:

"That dog cannot go on a shuttle." His accent, liltingly Indian, spoke of rules and regulations of a bygone era, the lingering aura of colonialism and its nascent delight in adhering to form, dotting the "I", keeping in step, and stiff upper lip, as he surveyed this ungainly, sweating crew of questionable people *and* their dog.

"What?" David felt like he would keel over.

"The dog, he must be in a crate. He cannot get on board my shuttle like that." Thin and dark, the shuttle raj drew out the last words with lingering satisfaction, the rule of the reign.

David pleaded, Barbara enjoined, they both demanded access, since *the dog had a first class ticket, better than most tickets, and would not be in a crate.* They shuffled the tickets in his face, fanned out like a poker hand, but he turned surly. "I don't care," and he moved to close the door.

Again, David yelled into a phone, calling the airport personnel as he checked his watch. The minutes did not lie — they would miss this plane, too. Another call, this time to the Leno people. The smooth, buttery voice of the Show Coordinator reassured him, with *don't worry, we'll get you from there to Los Angeles, we'll make the right calls. We are Jay Leno."*

As they stood fuming, flummoxed by events, with the Shuttle driver smirking as he drove away, a special van squealed up, doors flew open, and they were ushered in. "You're booked for a later flight," the attendant assured them, and for the distance of two miles — two blessedly calm, relief-filled miles — they kept the thought, "we are Jay Leno, we can make anything happen."

And just as they began to relax, the Dallas/Ft. Worth airport arranged another obstacle. The check-in line, merging with the boarding line, stretched in a serpentine curve nearly out the door. *A mile long and a day short,* David groaned, as he realized that they were never, ever, going to get to Los Angeles. And as if to underline this, a harried-looking official, pushing people out of her path to reach them, informed them that, because of the heat, the airline had an embargo on flying dogs.

Flying dogs? For a brief second, his eyes sought the ceiling to see any floating by, then realized that she meant dogs in the cargo hold.

" Ma'am, I am so exhausted. This dog has a ticket in first class, He is flying to the Tonight Show with Jay Leno, he is *on the plane* and *not* in the cargo hold. She seemed surprised, peered down at Skidboot, as if seeking signs of celebrity in the Blue Heeler with the red kerchief, and David wondered if he should add the shades. Skidboot looked oddly like Bruce Willis with dark glasses, and David fretted, remembering the sage advice of an elder cowboy who approached him at the National Senior Pro rodeo. "David," he said, "you got a great act with your dog. I was an extra in the movie *Shane,* and I got a good taste of movie life. You are going to get more and more popular, don't ruin it by going all Hollywood. People love the real *you,* not the celebrity stuff." David reached down and took off the glasses. There. His old pal, Billy, would be proud.

The attendant hurried off, and returned waving a paper wildly, like a fly swatter, shouting "follow me, follow me!" as they queued after her, a wedge formation cutting through the crowd like a football play as she announced, "celebrity status, please clear the way." Like ducklings, they trailed her to the head of the line, straight into the boarding area, and were waved through. Heads turned, people murmured, as they tried to register who or what had just gone through on its way to the NBC studios in Burbank, California.

"Skidboot, " David said, while buckling into comfortable seats, "you order whatever you want to eat, buddy. You get yourself the best." And within half an hour, Skidboot sat politely, waiting for Barbara to feed him, one bite at a time, as they sped toward their first encounter with Jay Leno and *The Tonight Show.*

By now, David and Skidboot had been on so many TV programs that the icy grip of fear had relaxed. David no longer felt dumbstruck, stomach-clutched and nerve wracked. He just tried to think sequentially, calmly, and identify the different performance segments. But first, he had to recover from the sight of Skidboot's dressing room, marked with a huge star and the words "SKIDBOOT."

The music rolled, the announcer announced, Jay Leno chuckled through a comic monologue, and then the guests popped in. He and Skidboot were number two, and they watched the action happen on the stage and overhead, onscreen.

I wonder if Skidboot knows what's going on? David thought. I hardly do.

They heard their names called, and suddenly, like magic, the two were cozily chatting with Jay Leno on the biggest talk show in America. David coolly gave Skidboot's lineage – Blue Heeler mother, scalawag father, address unknown. He told the audience how he'd threatened to get rid of the dog, he was such a miscreant, so badly behaved. How he'd finally trained Skidboot, even though he didn't know beans about dog training. Tonight, he threw in a segment about the truck.

"I have the drivers' license, not Skidboot. But the way he anticipates every move, it wouldn't surprise me if he drove off in it one of these mornings..."

Laughter. More laughter.

By now, Skidboot's performance path had veered from the usual Lion's Club or Kiwanis Club, from the rodeo circuit, from the church social and the school gym to venues of national dimensions. The first call from the Jay Leno show, although unnerving, kept pace with the rapidly accelerating pace of their lives. It was a magnificent success, far beyond anyone's imagining. And in later years, David had only one regret: that with Barbara in the audience, and the appearance happening on *her birthday,* that he'd never called her out, made national, televised mention of it. Nervous, he'd waited while the announcer panned through the opening credits, tapped his toes during the first monologue by Leno, smiled briefly at the comedy sketch and waited with trepidation for the first guest appearance – Skidboot. By then, the build-up of anxiety overflowed. He lacked the slick familiarity that show people develop in the camera's eye, the ability to chat, applaud and thank their sponsors. And no matter how many major appearances loomed, and how many precious people – including his wife on her birthday – that he failed to mention, he rationalized, thinking, *I'm just a horseshoer. But I'll learn how to do it better.*

CHAPTER THIRTY-ONE

Cruelty or Control

Leno had loved Skidboot the first time around, and the staff couldn't wait to have him back. On the second appearance, Leno knew only what he'd known the year before. What he didn't know about Skidboot was the back story, how the dog had gone "sour," how David had cooked up a mock rodeo to get him back on course, how Skidboot had fallen into a flare-up of rule breaking and rude surprises in front of a large audience, and how David Hartwig ended up doing the dance while his dog called the tune.

Leno didn't know this. All he knew was, that at Skidboot's second appearance, the dog had gone national and even had his own fan club. However, David still had to take a hand—from time to time—in making sure that Skidboot remembered the rules.

There was a camera on every floor of the Universal Studio building, and one of them had filmed David, this long, tall cowboy from Texas, throwing himself flat on top of the dog, growling like a grizzly in heat, pulling the dog's ears and yelling into his face. Typical backstage behavior for *humans,* not humans with dogs.

"Now David," Leno grew thoughtful. "You've been on this show before. We all love Skidboot, and respect the two of you greatly."

Skidboot stared at Leno. *You do?* Did Skidboot remember his first time on Leno's show? He recognized the bright eyes and the crescent chin of the big-time talkshow host, the man David was so excited about. No one in the audience had seen David's vigorous ear tweaking, only Leno. But Jay Leno knew that the monitor fed live coverage into the blue room where the board members congregated, and that one of *them* might have seen it.

They'd been warming up backstage, with David talking to his dog in a low voice, earnest, letting him know that this was a big afternoon. Assistants with untucked shirts and narrow eyewear kept them comfortable with water, snacks, Pepsi, whatever they wanted. David had turned to the technicians, the assistants, the camera crew, just to explain the ear-pulling agenda.

""I'm gonna warm up this dog a little. That means I *might* pull his ear, just a little, just so he knows that he can't cheat." He'd seen their glances. "Now, he may squeal, but don't worry." Again, the worried glances.

David had bent down to Skidboot. "You better behave! This is a big one. No cheating."

Skidboot shivered, delicious with anticipation. *Yes, a big one, we're here!*

But now came Leno, moving toward them, beckoning, smiling.

"Just a private word."

David bent his head to hear words that made no sense to him at first, in that they almost accused him of, what, mistreating Skidboot? He tried to fix on what Leno was saying. Bright lights nearly blinded him. A door slammed like a howitzer.

"...so please, David, don't intimidate the dog on stage."

The Jay Leno Show, America's favorite TV show, with America's favorite TV personality, bringing favorite segments to the American population, refused to associate with any kind of animal intimidation, even if it was "training."

David nodded, *now I get it.* They thought he was being cruel! Why, they didn't know about the long history of man and dog, the earth's first domesticated animal and its historic ascent to become man's almost-human companion. Both practical and familial, in Australia, the land of Skidboot's ancestry, the natives in the bush used dogs as blankets, burrowing beneath one, two, even three if the night was cold enough and giving rise to the term, *three dog night.* The bond of man and dog was longstanding, beginning with the dog's primary role up until the nineteenth century as a work beast, either hunting, herding or guarding. Cheerful empathy finally brought the dog inside the house as a tame family companion. As Susan Orleans writes, a wave of best-selling dog autobiographies were published in the 1800's, in which authors supposed what the dog thought and felt, giving the dog a voice in such bestsellers as *Memories of Bob* or *The Spotted Terrier:*

Supposed to Be Written by Himself. Here then were little quasi-humans even less powerful than their owners but compliant in every way, and besides, good company. Dogs, it was believed, had more empathy than people. Didn't they make incredible journeys to "find" a lost master or mistress? Didn't they mourn at a master's grave?

David and Skidboot had a working relationship. They understood each other. And no, he didn't favor the dog the way Barbara did, always trying to protect it, keep it comfy, see that it had treats and a lap to sit on. His relationship was more dominant: the big dog telling the little dog what for. David tried to convey it to Jay Leno, tried to reassure him, no ear-pulling, no human growling, nothing that might look like bully behavior on national television. Leno smiled, ever the host.

In all their career together, man and dog, David looked back on the Leno show as one of the two times the issue had come up.

The other happened half a year earlier, when he'd popped Skidboot with the piggin' string publicly to the horror of the rodeo committee. The gesture, as quick and surprising as a locker room towel snap, paralyzed Skidboot. He froze while licking his coat, stopped with his tongue halfway up his back. He eyed his own tail, then swiveled around and pointed his sleek head at the toy, eyes fixed, the mischief drained right out of him.

The rodeo committee knew that any roper worth his rawhide always carried his piggin' string, the most essential part of the roper's tool kit. This whip like leather thong up to 7-feet long, would tie the cattle's feet after roping. Some cowboys tie the string to a D-ring off the saddle, some tie it to their chaps, but wherever it lies, it's roped and ready. Work wise, the piggin' string comes in handy to as a slip knot around a gatepost to hold closed a wire gate if you can't make the latch fit. It doubles as a bridle rein, can hobble a horse and tie up a dog. The string, both ceremonial and useful, marked the owner, like Merlin's wand, as having power. *One pop with the piggin'*, said David, and Skidboot would behave. In fact, usually just the sight of the piggin' was enough to settle him into the routine. The piggin's power resided in action, as well as memory and symbolism. Only occasionally did he have to reintroduce Skidboot the hard way.

"They saw me being a little rough," David said, understanding how a group of people up in the control booth might wonder at him, a big man, throwing himself down in the *Growling Dog* exercise. "I get on top of Skidboot and just push him down," nearly flattening Skidboot but also giving him a feeling of security by being dominated. But the rodeo committee didn't like dog flattening. They recalled their own house pets, friendly Setters, Cocker Spaniels, bouncy and long-haired and companionable dogs who curled at your feet and fetched newspapers. No one had to flatten *their* dogs to get cooperation.

"No more of that rough stuff," they chided, and David reluctantly agreed.

One of the most important canine lessons is restraint, a master-doggie bargain usually struck during puppyhood. Skidboot, now age four, was past the teachable time, when a puppy's wobbly attention is focused with restraint devices such as a buckle collar. The trainer flops the pup up on a table or some place out of the comfort zone, then applies pressure as the puppy struggles, preventing nipping and biting by pressing a fistful of fingers under its jaw. The puppy can't bite, can't move its head, can't resist.

After a week or so of struggle comes compliance, rewards and more resistance, until the pup finally calms down enough for the next step, learning to lie on its side, called the lateral down. Methods differ, but a common approach might be to slide the dog down along the length of the trainer's body, holding its legs, praising it enough to calm the dog while correcting leftover, aggressive behavior. The training can last for months, but at the end, a relaxed dog is well-attuned to every inflection of the master's voice, to his or her movements, even expectations. Restraint, the pup learns, is unpleasant at best but, well, it *just keeps happening.* By teaching a dog to tolerate handling and to obey, it basically saves them stress. David knew that every dog owner, even those up in the stands, had thrown body blocks to tame a pet and were thus used to the idea of physical acts.

A dog, like any being, has choices and can choose *not* to cooperate. Since Skidboot had started his training late, his genetic qualities were sharply defined. A Blue Heeler, snarling and aggressive, is bred to *never quit.* A Heeler is a hard-headed, stubborn dog, a dog like a filibuster, a dog so tenacious it will fetch its own tail. You had to train them tough and damn the consequences.

"I am the meanest dog around," David snarled at Skidboot, "And 'cause of that, you don't have to be!"

Skidboot cocked an ear and studied David, his eyes pulled half-shut. He scanned the man's height, craning nearly up to the ceiling to catch the top brim of cowboy hat, the familiar one with the crease at the crown, then back down to the boots, slightly scuffed Acmes with square toes. *Really?* Skidboot pondered. *Maybe I need a hat too.*

No one needed to tell either one about empathy. Dogs, true empaths, are even known to be contagious yawners, copycats who see you yawn and join in. Which is to say, a dog can get as bored as a person. It was David's job to make sure that didn't happen to Skidboot.

CHAPTER THIRTY-TWO

New Dog, New Tricks

Contrary. That was Skidboot. Contrary. Also David Hartwig.

Even after the mock rodeos, the public punishment, the reluctant whittling away of Skidboot's ornery disobedience, David had a feeling that the dog's training lacked some hard underpinning, something bred of the wild that he hadn't been able to provide.

No one else thought so. Barbara, knee-deep in a job that took her 30-miles to work every morning and deposited her home late at night, spent more time driving than FedEx. She'd leave early, and David, looking around the empty house, would suffer the pangs—however brief—of the one left behind. A home guy, instead of the elite athlete he knew himself to be. Now, he was just the man who slapped together peanut butter sandwiches, packed lunch bags and swept up. He smiled at the thought, knowing it was only a partial truth. The real story lay in his work with Skidboot, an effort that was slowly, inevitably, transforming their lives.

"Hey, it's Skidboot!"

"Look, there's that dog!"

Everywhere he drove these days, people would wave at them, although mostly at Skidboot. Just a few years into the entertainment circuit and they were local celebrities! But something was missing…

David mused about it while shoeing, a steadily decreasing pastime now that they had the rodeo money. But it comforted him to have the heavy hoof bearing down, to trim and cut and hammer while puzzling out certain ideas.

"I got it!"

That day had started out with the Andersons pulling into the drive. People didn't often pull up, as the Quinlan property curled into cul-de-sac at the end of a long gravel drive. But when the UPS came, or the postman, Skidboot usually barked and pranced out to meet them. They would honk, a brief tap for politeness. In rural Texas, you never want to sneak up on anyone, it was only right to give a quick honk. In reality, the truck announced itself when Skidboot ran out, ragged howls of welcome flaking loose like paint chips. Then the cat yowled, the neighbor's chickens kicked in, messy little squawks, like "oh somebody broke my eggs! Oh be careful of the chicks." Followed by another dog or a nearby horse. The commotion spread like a rip tide, and this irked David. *Why do dogs always have to run out to the truck?*

Brilliant! He had a new idea.

Why not make Skidboot run to him first, a subtle master-trainee exercise that would turn the dog toward David first, the truck second. Subtle, he thought, maybe meaningless, but also, maybe not.

"I am going to reverse the natural order of things, " David told Barbara that night, to which she replied coolly, pulling Skidboot close and nuzzling him. "As long as you don't make it too hard on Skidboot. He works enough as it is."

He works? David thought. *What about me?* They both knew the unspoken rule, which was *anyone afraid of hard work had better leave ranching alone.*

Nighttime turned chilly even though it was mid-summer.

The next day, starting at daybreak, would be day one of Dog Reversal for David and Skidboot, an ambitious undertaking, but one that would cement the order between them. David placed his hands, large, square, able to lift half a horse if necessary, around Skidboot's neck. Softly, he spoke to the dog.

"Look here, from now on, you don't run after the cars and trucks. You don't go out barkin' when Barbara comes home. You don't announce yourself to the neighbors. Instead, Skidboot, *you come to me first!*

Inversion, or reversing the natural order of things seemed to David, well, natural. He usually reversed his own methods from what others thought tried and true. Life bounced with reversals. Why, he did it on the guitar and piano all the time, taking a Beatle's favorite, like *Here Comes the Sun* and modifying the melody to replace ascending intervals with descending intervals, or throwing in a bass note instead of a chord. Roger down at the hardware store always shouted out "water is precious, now you conserve," rather than "y'all come back, now." When pressed, he would murmur, "callighumpian," with no explanation. The man liked to play with words, reversing them—the way David played with music. It was unusual. Of course there were the usual salary reversals, when the bottom fell out of the pay scale. In any good book or play, events picked up when there was a reversal. Even chromosomes reverse themselves. Reversing the natural order of things seemed perfectly...natural.

So David worked with Skidboot, both falling into the familiar routine, the toy reward, the encouraging "good boy," the infinite number of checks and halts to get Skidboot to move slowly toward a toy, to stop, to hesitate, to tap once, then twice. David would murmur "tag my hand" or "tag my foot," and Skidboot, ears perked, would figure out the difference. The dog constantly amazed everyone, his skill verging over into inexplicable, because no matter how David mixed and matched the drill, Skidboot would understand it, would reach into the sorting and gathering part of his brain and match the command to the action.

Every success won him his toy, plucked from its storage place on the mantle. He loved sticks too, and the second David released him from his task and said "go get it," Skidboot would streak toward his reward, shaking the stick so violently that he kicked up dust, spinning in circles, slobber flying like a rainbird.

The training went on for a month, with Skidboot trying to run forward at cars and David holding him from behind. David was working with the natural instinct of the Blue Heeler, which was "herding" from behind. He sensed that it was sure to work out.

One evening, Skidboot heard Barbara pull up in her truck. Instead of the usual frantic "welcome home" yapping, he sedately stepped over to David, nuzzled his leg, pawed him once, twice and looked toward the truck.

"Yep, the truck's there all right. *This is unbelievable! A dog that doesn't bark at cars.* David stood wondering at the furry good fortune that had landed with them. A devout man who felt fulfilled by church on Sunday, he found only one explanation for their good fortune, and this idea — divine intervention — suited him just fine. This dog was a gift, come to improve their lot. Thanks were definitely in order. And Skidboot, for all he knew, had become a new inversion statistic, a thing that worked contrary to logic and pre-established order, much like the weather, the economy and the vicissitudes of the heart.

CHAPTER THIRTY-THREE

Team Skidboot

Oh no, David thought. Here he comes.

He tried to check the impulse, purely irrational, but he couldn't help pulling his hat down, nearly over his face. Skidboot looked surprised. Why was *his David* hiding his face behind the cowboy hat? This upset him, and he let out a quick bark. Face hiding wasn't part of their routine.

"Shut up, Skidboot!" David tried to turn their course from the sidelines, where they'd been watching a skilled roper chase down a calf at the Texas State Fair. David envied the roper, gliding like a charioteer, motions fluid, bandanna stretched out behind him in the wind. The freedom of it...

But there, right in front. Again! Randy Coyle.

Randy's eyes lit up when he saw them, and if he noticed that David was skulking with his hat pulled low, he neglected to mention it. Like all the ropers, Coyle knew about David's new calling, but what *he* called it was clowning.

"So, how's clown world?" David struggled to keep things light. He had an ongoing vendetta with this man, who won by hook or crook, using skill—*yes, he had skill* — nepotism and every illegal device he could find. Coyle was notorious for stuffing cotton in his horse's ears, sometimes used with skittish horses to help them focus, but seen in the rodeo arena as unfair advantage.

"I hear you're using tampons these days," David zinged, referring to the use of a tampon instead of cotton balls. The biggest joke in the rodeo happens when a tampon flies out of some mare's ear, making the crowd yell with laughter. A horse's ear is a strange, cavernous, crenellated area, the skin of the canal thick and slippery, filled with build-up, dirt and a rich supply of blood flow in the capillaries. Spooked horses are more spooked by having their ears handled, although any horse that gets *stuffed* as often as Coyle's did was probably used to it. For a tampon, you usually soak it with water, and it expands in the canal.

Coyle laughed easily, hardly bothered. "Whatever helps me win, my friend. And I'm doing a lot of that!"

Skidboot bristled, lifted his lip. He was on the verge of snarling when he felt David's hand touch his flank, one firm touch. He settled back and they walked away from the interaction, awkward, stiff-legged. David's familiar anxiety shot through him, his stomach lurched, he felt like heaving. It was one thing to ride confidently into the ring, familiar with the sway of Hank, knowing the feel of the rope as it sailed out of his fingers, falling into the body rhythm of a lifetime. But this was brand new. He had to depend on this dog not to be humiliated, and that was a lesson still to be learned.

Lord, don't let this go wrong shot through his mind, along with the realization that, trembling and anxious as he was, he couldn't even plead for success. He could only pray for the bare minimum, which was not to shame himself, himself, his family, and well, he guessed, his dog.

Indecision then vanished. A performer—no, two performers—entered the ring, greeted by an interested buzz. Any crowd gives a grace period as it waits, like a living thing, to be fed novelty, delight, and even surprise! Like children, they anticipate, and David felt a surge of responsibility. As part of this plan, he *would make it work.*

Gus, sweat streaming, shirt stained dark, bellowed over the mike, his words garbled into a stream as he *kicked off this year's annual rodeo talent show, mumble mumble, mumble.*

All David heard were the words "retired calf roper," which made him feel tired and defeated even before he began. They must have had the same effect on the audience, because the usual hush of anticipation broke. People coughed, chatter rose, interest flagged. Someone threw a beer can, and it bounced emptily on the pounded clay floor.

"...and his dog, Skidboot!!"

David wheeled around and saw Skidboot imitating his limp. "Not part of the show," he hissed, even though, later, he reflected on it and saw that it *was* pretty funny.

But not to the audience. They waited, deadpan, creating that inevitable entropy of disinterest that every performer shudders to encounter, although David was still too new to the entertainment game to really understand it. Still, Gus tried to drum up enthusiasm, his voice a carnival cry touting David's buckaroo past, calling him the best horseman yet, and asking—*was it begging?* —for a big welcome.

The applause drifted. People were waiting to see what this pair could do today, not what he'd done in the past.

Something propelled David forward, and within seconds, his natural storytelling nature took over. He hardly knew what happened. One minute, tongue-tied, asking the crowd if they wanted to see something funny, yet not even knowing what that was, to the next minute, when he threw the glove. Limp leather flopped into the dirt. Skidboot looked at it. David looked at Skidboot. The crowd watched them both.

"Now, I want you to bring me back that glove but only when I tell you to!"

So far so good. Skidboot gazed up at David, eyes like tacks.

"Folks, I don't even really know what this dog is. I think he's a Texas twister on steroids, but then..."

He interrupted himself. He spat out: "go – get- the - glove."

Skidboot shot forward, then David commanded, "wait right there." He was sweating with anxiety, worried. *If Skidboot doesn't stop, we're finished.*

Skidboot froze into Swing the Statue.

"Now go!" A cloud of dust.

"Now stop." Frozen in place.

The dog inched toward the glove, the man restrained him. Go, stop, go, stop, a medley of conflicting commands so perfectly orchestrated, but so continuous, that awe finally drifted into boredom. The crowd grew fitful.

Sensing this, David released Skidboot with a final "go, " except, no! Wait a minute! Skidboot had to tap David's right foot first.

Tap. Tap.

Skidboot quivered with eagerness, thinking *toy, toy.* And just as he was about to realize the toy, David quietly prevented it with "turn around."

What? Skidboot sensed that David was punishing him. This was too much, *he wanted the toy.* Grudgingly, Skidboot turned, following his tail as dogs have done throughout time, to make themselves into a perfect donut of a circle.

The crowd rustled, a living aggregate of diverse opinion, bleachered in layers around the arena like an inverted beehive, sweating in the sun, glistening with beer and popcorn butter. Heat rose off Skidboot's dark fur.

"Now the other way."

Gus, a showman who never missed an opportunity, tapped the mike, backed away from its sonic outroar, the buzz and crackle of a misfiring speaker: "so, David, how'd that dog know to turn the other way?"

"Well, Gus," David drawled, thinking *irresistible.* "I know you're from Oklahoma, but down here in Texas, once you've turned one way, there's only one way left to turn."

Laughter exploded, hoots, yells and boots stamping.

"Take a-hold!" David suddenly commanded, and Skidboot, sprung like an arrow, nailed the glove, gnawed it, pranced with it, snarled, head-butted David, and turned in a circle, wagging the glove wildly while the crowd cheered. Men and women struggled to stand, the sun glaring on shaded faces, everyone trying to get a better look.

The rest of the performance seemed like a dream, the concentration so palpable that once, David glanced at the crowded bleachers and jerked alert to see the wall of faces. *He'd almost forgotten where they were.* Like a surgical team, he and Skidboot passed ideas like instruments back and forth, David commanding and Skidboot quickly executing.

Suddenly, David yelled, "Look out, too much excitement! This puppy's gonna...oh NO, we got us a dead dog!" The crowd hushed as Skidboot tottered, teetered side to side, sighed and corkscrewed toward the ground.

David stood back in awe. Skidboot, the dog-mime, had perfected the facial expressions, paw signals and body motions of comic pantomime, developed by the Greeks, upheld in the medieval dumb show, paraded by silent screen actors Charlie Chaplin and Harpo Marx. In Skidboot, a critic might recognize the weirdly amusing staggers and lurches of French film actor Jaques Tati or the ubiquitous street theatrics of panhandler mimes. Skidboot seemed to be a dog for all seasons, all times and all audiences. David could hardly believe his eyes as Skidboot, like the masters before him, teetered, swayed, dragged out the fall for seconds, staggered gently and moved pitifully downward, eyes begging. The crowd exhaled at his final collapse.

David became King Lear mourning Ophelia, with *no, no, no life!..and Thou no breath at all?*

The "Play Dead" concept had failed a few months earlier, the memory of which still shamed David. But today was different, here in the Texas State Fair rodeo arena, "Play Dead" had taken on the solemnity of Aeschylus. Every eye followed the hero's downward spiral, a descent that the gods had promised but the dog had tried to resist, fighting with every drop of canine will until fate overcame and finally, with a "thump," he landed. His claws shot straight out, like chicken feet.

A roar of applause. They never thought he would fall.

David, looking long-faced and forlorn, gazed down at the fallen hero.

""Folks, we just lost him."

The crowd loved it. Someone yelled, "bring him back!" Like children, they wanted the magic, the age-old restoration of life to the lifeless, the *Lazarus* miracle.

David promised them that he'd try. He'd caught the drama of the moment, knew, like Skidboot, that it could be drawn out considerably, and with each suspenseful moment, their value on the rodeo circuit mounted. *This is getting to be fun.* He promised them that he'd give it his best, but he was just a rancher, just a cowboy, no apostle! He couldn't guarantee anything.

The crowd applauded, with yells of "bring him back!" "We want Skidboot!!"

David knelt beside the dog, a collapsed heap in the dust and begged the crowd for help. "CPR?," he asked, "Please?"

Gus, getting the gist, grabbed his speaker to beg the crowd for anyone, EMT nurse, Doctor, anyone who knew CPR.

"That's Cardio Pulmonary Resuscitation!" he yelled. One man half-stood in the stands, then his wife pulled him back down.

David, leaning over the stricken beast, looked up. "No sir," he said. "That's Cowboy Puppy Resuscitation!"

The crowd laughed as David leaned over Skidboot's corpse, gently pumping his chest. Once, twice, three times, until with no response, he bent down and blew into the curved, smiling mouth, thinking, *why do dogs always smile?* And he remembered how Skidboot had come up with this trick on his own, had understood from conversation what they wanted from "dead," what "dead" must mean, and had flopped over obligingly.

"Folks, it's not working." David pushed himself back up, forlorn. Then he brightened. "Let's try one more thing!"

"Skidboot, if you can hear me, touch my hand. Reach up, son, and touch my hand. David the revival preacher loomed over the corpse of the dog. "Just reach out!"

Skidboot weakly stirred, and the paw wavered up, searching, until it found David's outstretched hand. *Tap*, went the paw. *Tap, tap.* The crowd went wild, hooting, yelling.

Gus grabbed his microphone, "It's incredible, look at that, he's still with us!"

But David had more in store. He trusted Skidboot to follow up on the routine, and counted to three, telling him that if he *didn't* come back by the count of three, that he, David, would go ahead and bury him.

"One,"

"Two,"

Silence fell. David seemed like a serious type, and no one wanted to see a really dead dog.

"Three!"

Skidboot whirled in place on the ground like some kind of dervish, scattering dirt as he leaped to his feet and spun wildly around.

Gus squawked and buzzed his congratulations, people cheered, many yelled Skidboot's name. *Me?* He looked up, around the arena, seeing the people, hearing his name. *Me?*

Barbara and Russell were quickly beside him, and the family laughed, answered questions, hugged each other, hugged Skidboot, hugged Gus. David even heard Randy Coyle's comment as he walked by, a mumbled congratulations, and the question: *where did you ever find that dog?*

David smiled, hugged his family around him, and admitted that, thanks to time, circumstances, faith and good fortune, Skidboot had found them.

And as if that weren't enough, that moment of glory, of fanfare or bench-stomping festivity, another moment came as Gus pulled them aside. They were waiting for the final announcement of the grand prize for the year's rodeo talent contest. Gus, fascinated, queried David about *how on earth* he'd trained the dog, and David told him, concisely as possible, about all the afternoons when he and Skidboot would look up at the mantle filled with toys, how Skidboot would whine fetchingly, bat his eyes, paw at David and beg for a toy. And David would tell him, you *back up, and I'll give you a toy.* And the second Skidboot did anything that looked like backing up, even putting out a single reverse paw, David would jump up and fetch the toy.

"But only twenty seconds," David said. "That's the trick. You only wait twenty seconds. That's the learning window." Then up the toy would go to the mantle, then we'd start over again. "That dog has no quit," he told Gus. He will do anything, I mean *anything,* to get that toy."

Gus shook his head, amazed. Then the results came in; he flashed them a smile and made the announcement;

"David Hartwig and his dog Skidboot!" They'd won! $1,000 that would go straight to the kitty and would cleave away at the gas bill, the mortgage holdover statement and the partially-paid food tab at the corner store. All the little irritants that they couldn't pull out of the regular budget were fixed today by one dead dog.

They looked at Skidboot with mounting appreciation, although an irksome thought sprang into David's mind. *What about his real love, calf roping?*

CHAPTER THIRTY-FOUR

Horse or Dog?

The next day, David dug out his piggin', mounted Hank and released a calf into the family arena, a practice ring he'd used during his peak roping days. It had been a while, and Hank looked at him, deep and long.

"Get going, old friend," David muttered, riding him hard after the calf, jumping down, upending the calf and whip-tying the legs. He could only limp away, his leg was still bad. But limping wouldn't get him rodeo time, and when he checked the stop watch, he realized: *no way.*

Then he had another thought. If *he* couldn't rope and race like in the old days, what about Skidboot?

The phone calls were coming in now, but David knew the same old tricks weren't enough. The family tried to maintain its usual routine, horse shoeing, riding colts, and in the evening, Barbara would join David, riding in the practice arena. He would rope calves, and she would practice on the barrels.

Barrels.

Barrel racing is a girl's rodeo sport, an event for flashy young cowgirls in pastel western wear, lying low, fast and close to the saddle, to blur through a figure eight or the more contemporary cloverleaf. It's a mind crackling thrust of fast starts, faster stops and turns so quick that horsemanship is put to the test. A falter on either end, a break in the rider's mental focus, insecure footing, bit irritation, any distraction or disorganization that breaks the steely focus will lose clock time. Barrel racing is high drama, the rodeo's most popular event for cowgirl competitors.

The barrel race demands top speed. Horse and rider burst into the arena, knowing that every hundredth of a second counts. They flash across an electronic time beam and clock out at the end of the cloverleaf. The challenge is to maneuver a course in as little distance as possible by cornering the barrel; at a tight angle while the rider digs in knees and legs to secure the saddle. Instantly, directions switch, and the short distance — less than 100 feet — between barrels vanishes.

During practice, David noticed the dogs. Rodeo clowns send trick dogs in to skid around the barrels, pitching the crowd into laughter. Or, the cowgirls' dogs might dart into the ring during training sessions, fluffing and barking, and chase around the barrels after the horses. David couldn't understand how anyone could have a decent practice with the commotion of the dogs, and naturally, dogs were banned from the ring during the actual race. But it stuck in his mind. It gave him an idea.

Why not have Skidboot race barrels?

A barrel racing dog! The rodeos would love it, and it was time for the Hartwig show to expand its tricks. From idea to execution never took David long, and this time, he'd try and keep it simple by leading Skidboot around the first barrel with the usual temptation of a toy.

"Here boy, follow the toy!" David went twice around a barrel they'd set up in the ranch arena, enticing the dog with a stuffed rabbit. Around he went, once, twice. On the second circle David pitched the toy to Skidboot, who flew into his usual frenzy.

Good! David now had Skidboot thinking cloverleaf, as in *twice around to the right and I get a toy*, which led to the second barrel, which he cornered around, turning left. He hounded the toy like prey around the third and fourth barrels, with David flinging the toy as far as he could to complete the pattern and Skidboot leaping to intercept it, mid air. Successful, he'd howl, spin in circles, gnaw, gnash and explode with his usual uncorked, primal energy.

Barbara and David both howled along with him, yelling to encourage his wild behavior, while Russell, interrupted from studying, ran outside, watched the pair cavorting and shook his head. Studies called him back. *You can't get straight A's on luck.* He banged the screen door behind him.

David and Barbara slid glances at each other, laughed and agreed that it *did* seem crazy, but everything else seemed pretty mad, so why not go for it?

"Let's quit now, Barbara. I think he has the idea."

Thank you for noticing. Skidboot flicked his hindquarters David's way, a little butt toss to let him know he understood the drill. One thing both dog and man would say, if asked, is the importance of timing. Skidboot's quickness, the burner level of his mind, his flash of understanding, would have staggered into boredom by too much practice. David, also a quick learner, knew the drawback of overdoing it, and he never trained Skidboot past twenty minutes. Generally, Skidboot's learning curve was less than five.

The next day saw David pushing the big oak barrels around the arena, moving them closer, eying them to make sure there was still enough room for a healthy turn radius. Like an Easter egg hunt, he thought, as he hid a toy behind the first barrel, its stuffed paw barely showing. The barrel shielding the hidden toy lodged at the top of the first "leaf" of the cloverleaf pattern. Would Skidboot remember yesterday's moves?

The dog was lucky, really, since all he had to remember was four circles. A barrel racer would be nervously checking to see the size of the pen and how wide or long the alley was. They would have to scope out the alley to see if it was angled toward the fence or toward the first barrel, which would determine the direction. Was the ground too sandy? Could they keep their bodies on the outside or the inside leg while turning? They would review how far to reach down with the inside rein, how much pressure to put on the horse's mouth, how far to the outside to pull the horse's nose, whether the horse would catch his leads, and if he didn't, then improvise. They pad their shiny Bob Marshall saddles with impact gels for the rough ride ahead. Skidboot didn't have to consider any of this. He just had to remember his turns and think of his toy.

"Go git it!" unleashed Skidboot into his now-customary sprint. Slightly airborne, he stretched out lean as a greyhound, arching through the air to finish his routine without any further instructions.

"That is downright crazy!" The postman guffawed, watching. Neighbor kids leaned against the fence, wide-eyed. Barbara brought her horse over. And in a cluster of jeans, hats and stained western shirts, folks watched the crazy dog track David's commands, while David tried to trick the dog by slipping in new commands, enjoying how the dog began to understand them. Any athlete starts out at the bottom of the mountain, and by hard work and surprising perseverance, makes it to the top. David knew where he was going, but sometimes wondered if Skidboot was just a quick study or if he had ambition.

"You got to get that dog more venues," the postman nearly jittered with excitement. *You are reading my mind,* David jittered back.

CHAPTER THIRTY-FIVE

The Mystery Barrel Racer

Doug Williams, professional rodeo announcer, would officiate at the 53rd Annual Cooper Rodeo, which had launched on Saturday night with a cowboy supper by the Dutch Oven Cooks and a Western Swing concert. Few outsiders could understand the draw of a rodeo, but it reaffirmed values and upheld the ranching nostalgia for those who idealized it and who found ways to celebrate their addiction in every small rodeo that popped up in every state west of the Mississippi. Eager contestants moved from one to the next, unconcerned about the rodeo's size or even the prize, but just for the opportunity to show horsemanship.

The Cooper rodeo, although relatively small, drew wranglers and cowgirls from Northeast Texas, Oklahoma, Arkansas and Louisiana to the high thrills of barrel racing, breakaway roping, bronc riding, team roping and bull riding. Tiny Cooper's motto was "we are a small county in northeast Texas, and we can live with that." In addition to a lake, thirty one square miles in size, Cooper could always brag about its rodeo.

A steady stream of horse trailers drew up, raising puffs of smoke like a frontier round-up. Doug watched them gather beneath the shade of the trees, drivers unfolding from behind the wheels, tugging belts, hats, greeting friends. One of the lesser attractions of the Cooper rodeo was the large, tree shadowed grassy area offering tasty grazing for the horses, as well as a bouncy soft cushion to stand on. A small thing, but small things often made the difference.

Doug had been doing this long enough for it to fall into a routine, which was why he was surprised when his producer told him to hang tight, there was a surprise coming on Sunday afternoon.

Surprise? He didn't like surprises. He couldn't really announce a surprise if he didn't know what it was, now could he?

No, he was told. Doug would *like* this surprise, just get ready to announce it around barrel racing time.

So here he stood, relieved that the day was perfect, the crowds happy, the sky a spry blue. He checked his schedule, seeing the usual line-up, Janna on Whiplash, Cissy Sparks on Lulu, Meg Hotckiss riding that feisty and well-named Cross Purpose. All were competent and would give a tight race to the finish, delighting the rodeo fans.

Then he studied the line-up, saw a new name and frowned. Was this the surprise? He didn't like not knowing. Usually he spun out a little biography before each pair entered to show his own expertise as well as giving the girls a minute to relax before show time. But this one....he shrugged. Guess he'd just call out the name. But wait, he studied the list again. Who was the rider?

Again, he shrugged. He'd been told to expect a surprise, and this must be it. He let it drop, since the powers-that-be had sent it through and probably knew what they were doing.

Almost time. He turned and strode toward the arena, as sun-struck as everyone else, his hat pulled down to create shade and his stained shirt loose. No one ever failed the regulation dress code at a rodeo, and he was no exception.

"Ladieeees and gentlemen, we have the most popular event of the rodeo today, the cowgirls' competition, the time to see the pigtails fly, the horses corner, and the barrels roll!" Doug prided himself on repartee, always looking for a lively phrase, like "pigtails." He slid his gaze around to see if there *were* any pigtails.

The girls wheeled, raised dust, cornered, reined and cornered again, laying so low in the saddle as to be almost invisible. The horses also planed in at the same flat angle, so that any upset, any misstep, any distraction — even the buzz of a horsefly — would collapse them into an unfortunate pile of legs, hooves and broken spirits. Miraculously, this seldom happened. The girls maintained the impossible angle at top speed, bringing the crowds to a standing cheer at each near miss.

He checked his watch. Nearly 3:30, about time to wrap up. But no. One more thing. He hated announcing blind.

"Folks, we have a late entry to the barrel racing. His name…is Skidboot!" *There, he'd done it.*

All eyes swiveled to the horse stalls, expecting a mounted gelding to burst through. Instead, a lone cowboy, booted and somber, strolled into the arena.

Doug tried to shoo him away, "Sir, you need to get out of the way. We got a high speed contestant in the wings, it's dangerous out here."

The man tipped his hat, "yes sir, it *is* dangerous. We live in dangerous times. And I, for one, am going to stand back, because...

Then he yelled, "ok, let her run!"

The crowd sighed, a collective intake, as if clouds had shifted before a storm as a black-and-blue animal shadow shot into the arena, smaller than a horse and faster than most dogs. Skidboot didn't even glance at David, not pausing for him or for the crowd, just flashing like a bolt toward the first barrel. He rounded it, speeding as flat to the ground as a race horse, headed for the second barrel, turned it and sped straight down the length of the cloverleaf turn for the third barrel. As the crowd yelled, stomped and went raucous, he hairpinned around the last barrel and skidded through the sand to intercept the toy that David lobbed at him. A twist like a caught fish, and he nabbed the toy in midair, shimmied right, then left, then right again, almost maniacal with growling, snarling, slobbering, ripping—his usual insane toy behavior. The crowd loved it, and after several savage minutes—with the toy shredded into wads of cotton, blue velour and a lone rabbit ear—David broke Skidboot into his routine of tricks: fetch, count, paw and reward.

The applause deafened David, who tried to reach down and touch Skidboot to prevent some kind of fear reaction. Here were a thousand people standing up in the stands, stomping, hollering and yelling. David had no idea if the crowd would terrify Skidboot—it certainly had caught David off guard. Skidboot's half smile cracked into a widespread dog smile, so large that no one could mistake his excitement. He slowly rotated his head around, up and down, scoping out the yelling masses. You could almost hear his thoughts, *I like this.*

David commanded Skidboot to turn right. He turned.

Then to turn again. And he did.

Then turn back again. And he did.

Williams' face shone with excitement. *This is pure magic,* David thought, drawing the moment out, savoring it. *Even I'm impressed.*

After, when David placed 9.4 in the calf-roping competition and bagged a nice pile of prize money, he and Skidboot looked at each other, two performers bringing home their wages. The family not only had a dog but another breadwinner. Barbara and David would freely share this role with anyone, dog or human. Barbara had lost her job and was looking daily for something else. Now, with Skidboot and David performing, it meant bills paid, Russell's books bought, an occasional chicken dinner out, gas money, non-stop electricity and heat— simply, life as they wanted it.

Barbara, always Skidboot's champion, wrapped the Heeler in a tight embrace, his narrow face turned up toward her, his eyes bright and appealing. Times felt good for the Hartwig family. The chickens were laying, the rodeos were paying and the neighbors flocking around them, intrigued by the afternoon practice sessions—they'd rather watch the Hartwig circus than bale hay! So good, in fact, that David could almost remember their courtship days. But time and troubles drifted in, a smothering thing, hardly recognizable. What seemed like family stability began to feel like military entrenchment, not the sustaining union it was meant to be. But now, in the pure excitement of their success, tenderness welled up. If they were not the family that prays together—Barbara resisted being part of that loop—at least they were a family that stays together.

CHAPTER THIRTY-SIX

The Trials of Fame

"David! Telephone!"

Daily, a new call. Newspaper interviews, TV stations and now, The Texas State Fair in Dallas *again,* wanting them as full-time entertainment. Errol McCoy called him first when he was in Charlottesville, Pennsylvania, on a dog-and-rodeo tour. "Think it's about time we make a deal," McCoy said. "Come in and talk."

Not just a one-time appearance, but a contract for every single day of the fair or almost a month's worth of income. David tried to imagine how hard he'd have to work to make this kind of money shoeing horses. And they were not even arena performers, which would be hard work. No, this was just *walking around,* doing a few tricks in an offhand way, gathering crowd interest, being Mr. Hospitality with his dog—a State Fair personality.

David put on his math hat. After the past two years, he'd grown more bold with the numbers, seeing in their growing celebrity a one-time opportunity to net profit. As an exercise, he'd dream up the most improbable amount and throw it out, just to see the reaction. David loved to gauge reactions, and if they went for it, well...

He needed a hundred dollars a day, yes sir.

A hundred a day, he was almost embarrassed to ask. *A hundred dollars a day just to strut through the aisles playing with his dog.* He wobbled mentally for a minute, unsure.

"You got it," Gus said, not a moment's pause. When David explained the job to Barbara, she, too was confounded.

"Not the floor show? Not in the arena?"

"No, and listen to this. We just walk up and down the street four times a day and do about five minutes of tricks!"

He turned to Skidboot. "That's $2,400 for just hanging out!" Skidboot barked, *2,400 what?*

Pure euphoria. There prevailed a sense of *rightness,* which so often turns into self-worth or even callous disregard. It lands gently, an insidious and subtle feeling, hard to resist. It plucks the juicy fruits of success and turns it soft around the edges.

When Butch knocked at the door of the mobile home — *bang, bang* — David felt a chill of inevitability. The sight of his friend, broad-faced, sunburned, ever-friendly, conflicted David. Butch was one of the few people who understood that if anything special was going to happen in Quinlan, it would happen to David. He'd seen David build his own horse stalls, thresh his own hay, puzzle over building his own pump, wire his own house. He never saw David require anything from anyone else, except maybe that sad night before Christmas when he'd run out of gas money. David was a fix-it polymath, which was why Butch had come to call.

"Got a few horses needin' your services, David. Think you could fit me in?"

There. He'd said the words they'd both been dreading, because now David had to shuck and sputter and finally blurt out "no." That is, no, he wouldn't be doing any work, not now or not—possibly—ever. Things with the dog, you know. Complications. Performance obligations…

He trailed off, seeing Butch's crestfallen face.

"Sure wish you might of told me sooner." The moment, brief in time, tested friendship against need and utility, and the two men, whose natural impulse of help and share was pushed sideways by this deliberate calculation, edged away from each other. David would remember the moment, as Butch studied the backs of his hands, flecked and corded by work, sun and time, his eyes locked down as if each scabbed knuckle bore information. This moment would haunt them, try their friendship.

Then Butch jammed his hands in his pockets and persisted. He hoped David could do it just this once, as Butch was in a bind, well, nearly an *emergency.* The county had more horseshoers than horned toads, *you just kick the bush, and out they come,* David once said. But many of them were part-time, poorly-trained men who thought they could turn a dollar by blasting the cracks off a hoof, need it or not. Others showed off their high-tech equipment, designed to scare owners into paying high prices, but, according to David, were "all hat, no cattle." Instead, David Hartwig paraded a low-tech, competent approach along with a casual billing attitude, as in, *if I can get paid, so be it.* Few of the locals could do David's work as quickly or as well. His hoof wall restructuring set a record — like calf roping, he had perfected performance horse shoeing.

The men faced each other, both embarrassed. "No" hung in the air, pushing friendship, proximity and generosity aside. One said "no," and the other countered with *I'd consider it a favor.* The words stonewalling till they dropped as the men turned from each other, Butch shifting down the steps as David retreated into the safety of the mobile home, his heart gone spastic.

What am I thinking?

The phone shrilled, jerking him toward a Checkovian world of strange complexity, where requests, buzzing neighbors, compliments, interviewers and well-wishers merged, nonstop. The State Fair people clamored, then Russell called, eager to talk to Skidboot and, excited, began to spin off tales to his dog pal about college, his interest in the law — *law, you know what that is, Skidboot?* — about going out last Saturday night, the people he'd met, while Skidboot, earnest as a professor, bobbed his speckled head, nodding "yes, yes, yes." His faraway look gave credence to Russell's eager words, he keenly recognized the tinny long-distance tones of his boy, Russell. Finally, he growled softly, *rrr-rrr-fff!* — Then:

"See ya later!" Russell to Skidboot.

"Rrrrr," Skidboot ended the call.

CHAPTER THIRTY-SEVEN

Riding Shotgun

Beautiful women didn't turn his head. Clothes, a good watch, fancy riding gear didn't tempt him.

But David lusted, nevertheless. And the lust that had lain dormant all those years of scraping along, suddenly surfaced. He was flooded with craving, excitement, deep interest and a longing so unexpected that the only thing he could do was stomp the brakes, prompting the usual moaning of mixed gears and cracked brake pads as Skidboot flew headlong into the dash.

He wondered, briefly, how such a smart dog could lose his seating so easily, as David broke his headfirst tumble with a stiff protecting arm, keeping Skidboot from head trauma. Man and dog sat silently in the dented truck, one transfixed, the other puzzled. David had come to rely on his cockpit buddy, nose pointed straight windward, ears flapping like mini propellers. All he had to do was think "drive" or "go" or "truck" and Skidboot was already there, vibrating in place by the closed door, whimpering with excitement. He loved the truck and would turn to David and ratchet up his smile in a show of happy teeth. *Yes, yes, let's drive, move it, more speed!*

Skidboot shook with excitement if David even *looked* at the driveway or at the old pickup, so dinged, faded and encrusted with use. Anywhere else, it would be an embarrassment. Here in Quinlan, it just said *hardworking and not too lucky.* But to Skidboot, "truck" meant adventure, a way to make the world slide by at high speed, to prickle his fur with blasts of hot Texas air.

"Skidboot, look at that, buddy!"

Skidboot looked. He saw the object of David's passion, and he, too, was dazzled. Imagine, *a new* truck as bright as Lake Tawakoni in the sunset, with gleaming silver insignia and mysteriously darkened back windows that seemed to wink at him, slyly. A new truck could be incredibly fast. It could purr like the great beast that it was and finish with a roar. David, in a trance, followed his heart into the dealership, sat down, had a talk, watched the miracle figures of his credit dance across the screen, said "yes," signed papers, and still in a daze, drove home.

Skidboot seemed to like the new Ford King Ranch with a crew cab and burrowed, pawed, scratched and sniffed around, taking it all in. But his place was at the window, nose pressed to the glass, until they sped up the gravel drive to the mobile home. Then, the euphoria began to trickle away, a change in mood that Skidboot felt. They still had to tell Barbara, who might have her own plans for their newfound income.

David slowly unwrapped himself from the truck and slowly stealthed inside. He hoped she wasn't home.

Barbara guarded the screen door.

"Honey, I got us a little surprise..." David edged toward the trailer.

The door slammed closed. David turned and took another look at the truck. *A man has to get around dependably,* he told himself, hoping that he was being honest.

CHAPTER THIRTY-EIGHT

What a Real Dog Trainer Would Do

The first day of the Texas State Fair proceeded like any other: hot white skies, perspiring barkers, red-faced vendors and an elemental hum of anticipation that droned like a hive. The Anderson family, just in from Pecos to visit relatives in Dallas, had paid their money and were heading for the famous Ronald McDonald show when Clinton, age 9, tugged his father's arm. "Dad," he whispered, "look over there."

All heads swung toward the pointed direction.

They saw the man, tall and seemingly disinterested. Swirling around his feet was a sparkly looking black and blue dog, real alert.

"What, son?" Nothing special there.

"Watch!"

The man strolled along casually, then pointed out a litter of trash, *over there!* The dog responded by pouncing on the litter and bundling the wrappers and a tin can in his jaws and trotting over to a nearby trash box. He hoisted himself up to the top and dropped them in.

"Jim, did you see that?" Angela and Jim hurried to catch up, and as they did, several others swept up behind them. Eager whispers, disbelief, as the man and the dog continued down the parkway, taking in the sights, no hurries, no worries. Only every time a can glinted, glass glittered or paper rustled, off went the dog to retrieve it. Within minutes, the crowd had grown, people were murmuring, wondering.

This should be entertainment, someone said.

Why, it already is, someone else answered. And each time the dog retrieved, the man very politely thanked him.

"Thank you, Skidboot," he said. Soon, the followers were murmuring, "thank you, Skidboot," as the pilgrimage wended toward the "Birds of the World" pavilion. Plans were dropped, mouths hung open. This trash collecting dog was a first.

Then the man started to vary the routine, perhaps conscious of the attention, although he kept his hat pulled low and seemed not to notice the growing crowd behind him. "Skidboot," he instructed as the dog went loping toward a torn newspaper. "You stop now."

The dog froze.

Everyone stared.

Then, gently, he released the dog. "Ok, sneak up on it now." Skidboot hugged the ground, a canine commando inching toward the trash.

"No," the voice insisted. "Back up now, too close."

The crowd felt more and more irritated. Why won't he just let the dog get the trash?

"No." "Back up." "Now go." "No." Under the flurry of commands the dog lay, crept, retreated, crept again, froze, retreated and advanced, as choreographed as a western line dance. Tension sparked through the crowd, they wanted this dog released!

Finally, the order, "go get it!" and Skidboot leaped forward, only to freeze in place with the following, "just touch it, now." The dog reached out a paw and ever so delicately, patted the trash.

"Ok, Skidboot, now you go get it." Palpable relief flowed as Skidboot careened toward the huge trash drum, scaled it like a rock climber and dropped the trash inside.

The Anderson family phoned their friends the Oddwaters, who were meeting them at noon and urged them to find the Bird Show area, there was a trick dog wandering around that they shouldn't miss.

David and Skidboot tried to wrangle free, but crowds pressed in, people asking for another trick, to pet the dog, to find out who they were, and by the time they fought their way free, David felt worn out. They "strolled" three more times that day into different parts of the fairground, trying new tricks, improvising. Around noon, stomachs growling, David spotted a hot dog stand.

Why not have Skidboot buy him a hot dog? He and Skidboot seemed to have the same thought at the same time, and just as Skidboot started toward the stand, David remembered to "instruct" him to go get them a hot dog.

The vendor, accustomed to human faces, peered down at the eager canine, then over at David, who gestured, hot dog please. The vendor, Marie, laughed. She'd never seen anything like it, but noticed right away that the dog was good for business. The minute he trotted off, the hot dog held delicately in his mouth, about fifty people all wanted "hot dogs like the dog had," which caused Marie to think *one good dog deserves another* and she threw in a free one—no condiments since he disdained relish or mustard—for Skidboot.

CHAPTER THIRTY-NINE

The Pied Piper

By the end of the day, David was bushed. Like the Pied Piper, he trailed a line of people. He wasn't even sure this was his assignment—to just wander around, playing with his dog—and this made him nervous. He didn't want to jeopardize the $400 he'd make today.

Just then a burly man planted himself in front of David, and he glimpsed the official badge swinging from his neck.

"Sir," he said. "You two are causing a lot of commotion."

David's stomach dropped. He knew he'd forgotten something, gotten off into the wrong area or had a time conflict—he'd had this bad feeling. He gulped, apologized, kicked the dirt with his boots, held onto Skidboot's neck, ruffling his fur, feeling the familiar vibration of excitement ripple along his back. Skidboot loved a strong caress, the probing fingers that worked around on his muscles, stroked his neck, grabbed his chest fur, pulling and playing.

"People are calling up the fair, talking about you and the dog."

"Sorry, we were just..."

"Sorry? By Gosh, no need to be! We've had so many calls that management made the fastest decision I've ever seen at the Fair. They're hopin' you two can be regulars here."

He paused. "As long as the dog is healthy and so forth..." They turned to look at Skidboot, whose bright eyes and bristling fur brimmed with vitality.

"You mean..." David's confusion left him almost speechless.

"That's right. Every day. You get the same pay, $400."

Like a human calculator, Skidboot looked up at David and began to pat his knee lightly with his paw. Was he counting? David was. And 400 times 30 days turned out to be more than he could fathom. And just for playing with the dog.

They shook on it, agreed that the contract would come later, while Skidboot rippled up and down with excitement. Balloons floated up from the Midway, and the bright colors of the day turned into a carnival of light, sound and frolic, as if angels were playing nearby, whispering his good fortune. David paused a moment to try and understand why such luck would come his way. He had no idea where it was headed, but he liked this new direction better than anything yet.

"Thank you, Skidboot," he whispered, grabbing Skidboot's staunch little shoulders, pulling him close.

The day proceeded, and then the day after, as the pair turned into regulars who dragged along behind them, a wedge of humanity—the people who followed the dog show. In the way that adults love children, they loved the dog. In the way that parents see themselves as models and trainers, they identified with David's brand of dog guidance. People tried to figure out where they'd be next. They would spread the word, and daily, the crowds grew.

By now, both David and Skidboot were less edgy about confrontation. The last run-in they'd had with an official had ended well—*with increased benefits!*—so when David saw the thin man, well-pressed, striding toward them, he gave it little thought. But after the first words, he shuddered to realize that this was a professional dog trainer, come to tell him his mistakes and tear apart his techniques.

"Been noticing you and the dog," the man began, self-effacing, keeping his distance.

"Um-hm" David noticed that, like two dogs, they were circling and sniffing. One of us is gonna pee first.

"Wonder if you've been using Clicker training? I notice that your dog responds to hand gestures.

"Um-hmm."

The man dropped the self-effacing role and moved in for the kill.

"You know, there's an entire school of discipline that I myself promote, it's purely positive motivational training, using rewards to reinforce good behavior. It's based on Thorndike's Law of Effect, which says that actions that produce rewards tend to increase in frequency and actions that do *not* produce rewards decrease in frequency. We use an assortment of crates, tethers and head halters. It seems to me that your dog here might benefit from some reinforcement."

And so would you. David felt unkindness well up, as well as unease. These professionals were always turning up, and he should have spotted this one. They were compelled to offer him tips on training and point out what he'd been doing wrong. David had one response.

"Mister, I am not a dog trainer and this dog is not trained. I'm just playing with my dog, that's all. He and I get on together. All I look for in a dog is good manners."

Then, making a small shoving-aside gesture, which really didn't touch the man but just cleared the path, David and Skidboot circled out from the heat of his analysis, suggestions and weighty schooling, and made their way down toward the Texas Skyway, the five-million-dollar gondola that transported Texas State Fair revelers from one end to the other.

By the time the third hombre had planted himself in front of David, official tags dangling, he was used to it. Oh well, he thought, we're either washed up or in spin cycle, might as well relax. He'd always been opinionated, and no telling who he'd offended. So he smiled, shook hands and waited for the complaints. Instead, he heard that Mr. McCoy, the producer of the Texas State Fair, wanted to see David in the office, pronto. And the meeting that took place, pronto, was a surprise.

"David, we've got a problem with you walking around this way."

David's heart lurched. The idea of losing this job, the money, the fun of it saddened him. But life had prepared him for any vicissitude, and he'd handle this one. He could go back to horseshoeing and be perfectly happy, why he could...

"People are calling up the fair office all day long."

"Oh, I'm sorry about that," David shuffled his boots, first the left, then the right.

"Sorry? They all want to see you and this dog! Why, we've got more calls for the two of you than anything else at the fair."

More than clowns? More than the Texas Star Ferris wheel? More than Fletcher's brand corny dogs? Or, incredibly, more than the oddity of batter slathered, deep-fried coke?

The sheer incredulity of his position struck him, a hard cerebral slap. How long would it be before they realized he was just a cowboy with a cowdog having fun? Yet this was beginning to sound a lot like the earlier conversation that landed him a full-time job. What now?

Mr. McCoy strode around his desk, clapped his arm around David's shoulder and breathed heavily at him. The Fair wanted them as regulars, ones with a booth so that people could *find* them. Why, there would be three fifteen-minute shows each day, THREE, he practically shouted, as if anticipating an argument.

David swiftly calculated, only three a day was less than two-hours work for the same $400! Of course they might go into overtime, and then he'd spend time getting to and from the booth, not to mention lunch and snacks, but the sheer craziness of playing with his dog for less than two hours a day for that kind of pay was incredible. This was life, with all its unexpected upswings.

McCoy, as if talking to himself, crooned, "and we'll put up a sign, and some Astroturf, and rope off the area...we'll hand out flyers, give directions in the regular brochures." He laughed. "My boy, you are gonna be a star!" David looked around, not sure which of them he was talking to.

CHAPTER FORTY

Crowd Control

The fantasy continued. Spring turned to summer, bringing its usual changes to North Texas. The cottonwoods shone with oozing sap, and the round green pods of the trees would soon be trailing wisps of cotton. The willows, thin and whippy, were nearly leafed out, and Drake mallard ducks patrolled the streams leading from Lake Tawakoni. Soon ducklings would frisk, and the mating calls of magpies and the pie-billed grebe would sound. Texas has more wild birds than any other state in the Union, and spring seemed to bring them all out.

Daily, David and Skidboot left their trailer to breathe in the soft scents of each new morning. After that came hair-combing, shirt-tucking, coat-grooming and coffee-slurping. Then they would dive into the crowds of festival junkies flopping with cowboy hats, jostling with kids and pets. A flotsam of jolly fair wear—flared shorts, thigh-cut jeans, cool guy Panama hats, Armani eyewear—was borne along by a murmuring, slurping, ear bud-plugged crowd. At times it eddied and clogged, then swelled, then grew nearly impenetrable. And only with difficulty did they manage to shinny and squeeze their way through to the booth. David had to body block his way once, then tap a man's back with "excuse me..."

Suddenly, the sea parted with, "Look, it's them, it's Skidboot!" The chatter rose, spiraled, grew. This crowd thronged around them.

It amazed David that they had fans. And that these fans collected into crowds, and the crowds became sprawling, ragged flocks that that would call him by name, know his story, anticipate his dog's tricks, and swarm him, as if he were Mick Jagger. His solitude was shattered. Publicity violated every principle by which he normally lived, yet now shaped his days, defined his performances, skewed his relationship with his dog and his family. And here, a crowd so overgrown he couldn't fight his way through it. His ears rang with applause as the plurality flowed around him, edging closer to see the dog and the cowboy—him! They were like Black Friday shoppers, and he was...well, Macy's or the Apple store.

"Look, it's him!"

Squeals, pushing, autographs begged, photos demanded, hurried requests, whispered praise, stories blown about by a blizzard of humanity. Skidboot planted himself firmly at David's knee. In herding, when cows were scattered over the range and the cactus might harbor a rattler or two—the calves would mother up, their small shapes tucked into the large safety of the mother. David was no mother, but he felt Skidboot mother up to him anyway, and he knew why.

CHAPTER FORTY-ONE

The Late Show with Letterman

The Letterman show both reflected society and was shaped by it. Like the State Department, it sucked in baseline research and spit out policy, each policy being the groundwork of a new show. A serious man, Letterman wanted to be relevant, and was.

Outsiders might be daunted by the sheer complexity of the operation, the control rooms, the jungles of audio/video equipment and the cutting room spinning out five polished performances a week. There were remote production trucks jammed with video and audio cable filming the onstage cast and chorus, while the TV rehearsals and taping took place at the Ed Sullivan Theater on West 53rd Street, where audiences clapped on cue, excited to be part of the New York scene.

The Letterman Show had racked up countless prizes for Outstanding Variety, Music or Comedy, but prestige aside, the show was only as good as it's research team, an ultra-educated, hyper-driven and over-caffeinated hive of media specialists who begin each day by scanning every newspaper, magazine, radio transmission (today blog or tweet), no matter its size or following, from the Muleshoe *Journal* on. They take note of DJ patter, watch the dawn after late-night talk shows, then scour nationwide info waves, searching for the new and the different.

If a small town mayor made an election joke, they heard it. If Faith Hill flubbed a Country Music award, they took note, amassing talking points for the Letterman nightly monologue, as well as show and category ideas. Categories ranged from kid scientists to stupid human tricks, but the category that drew in David Hartwig was "Stupid Animal Tricks," which brought a riptide of oddities before the camera—a Bulldog on a rocking horse, a devil-possessed Japanese miniature lapdog dressed in Chanel, a double-Dutch rope-jumping cattle dog, one mutt who turned into a canine coffee table and balanced a cup of water on his butt, and even Misha, a Corgi who blew bubbles underwater.

There seemed no end to the oddball antics rehearsed in homes around America, and David Letterman let his staff know he was interested in seeing them all. Why not have auditions?

The quest was three good "stupid" tricks, but after days spent sweltering in a Dallas auditorium, tempers had frayed, dogs were hyperventilating, cats were catatonic, and the line of interviewees still lined up until Sunday. And worse, despite the heat, the crew found that Texans ate nearly everything chicken-fried. Head producer Cal Finer even found *mayo* on a salad. No one from New York ate mayo, and he finally had to get his assistant to buy a metal strainer and *wash his salads* before eating. He equated bread and barbecue with the beer-belly locals out walking the streets.

Morning number three, Finer received good news:

"So, you're saying we already have the trick?"

"Um-hm"

"Excellent!"

They stared at Skidboot and David, who had run through their standby tricks without missing a beat. Any concerns about the dog's showmanship vanished amidst the confusion of staff, crazy cameras and more lights than Christmas, proving that this dog could hold under fire. Even when the film crew moved in, a fly cam hoisting a 40-pound camera on a stabilizer that nearly flattened Skidboot, the cam driver yelling back something, maybe an apology. People shook their recording devices like rattles. David heard "pan" and "paint" and maybe "tilt," but by their turn, peace seemed to flow as David took a big step forward, and Skidboot mimicked him. Syncopated as twins, they moved, shadowed each other, David taking one step, Skidboot another, as they shuffled together, turned backwards, turned in reverse, held a leg up, a leg down, even to the point of David dropping to all fours and crawling, after which Skidboot also went infantry. He crawled along the floor, mimicking every pause, slide, grimace and pant. David finished with a superb roll over, nearly colliding with Skidboot's own identical maneuver. Their only difference seemed to be that one had a fur coat he could shake out, the other did not.

"You and that dog are downright unbelievable...and you know, this is high stakes, here. High Stakes," Finer said. Hartwig and his dog would find this out soon enough.

Don't Call It 'Stupid Pet Tricks'

They were selected. And after the call came, Skidboot and David capered around, laughing, trying a few Square dance turns. They'd had excitement for a while now but nothing as big as a trip to the Letterman show in New York.

"Let's just not say 'stupid tricks' around Skidboot," David said. He never considered anything they did together as stupid.

"Of course not!" Barbara concurred. Like the epic Rin-tin-tin, he was a high-level intuitive who needed to be doing useful work, not "stupid animal tricks."

But still...New York!

The day dawned calm, with a glowing sky and the confused cry of a barn owl settling into sleep. Skidboot bristled and paced, eager to get out and herd cattle.

"Not today, boy," David encouraged, gently, "today is fly day." Inside, David quaked, nervous about the upcoming event and the long flight. David became claustrophobic thinking of it.

Barbara still rummaged for the keys, but the minutes were ticking. "Any luck?" David shouted, getting edgier.

Finally, when the cab, the run to the airport, the adjusting, the tinkering was over, he woke up in New York, ready to burst out into the brisk air and get back to normal.

"Look at that, Skidboot!" David knew Barbara would have loved this; too bad she couldn't come. He sighed again, braced to the cold wind, and like true men of the range, cowboy and cowdog marched out to meet their fate.

CHAPTER FORTY-THREE

Roll, Fetch and Meet New Fans

The Mayflower Hotel, one of the oldest, most comfy yet venerable New York hotels held itself haughtily on New York's Park side, an 18-story, 365-room faded socialite designed by Emery Roth in 1926. It still clung to past elegance, even though parts of it were now a residence hotel. Hewn of vintage stone, its artful brick palisade ran along Central Park West, offering a dignified contrast to such glitzy architectural newcomers as the bronze mirrored Trump Towers or the upward swoop of the Time Warner Center nearby.

Visitors admired the façade of the old hotel, with its plaque commemorating the site as the 1898 birthplace of Vincent Youmans, the composer of "No, No, Nanette." Their heads swiveled up to view the cut-glass chandeliers in the lobby, the bronze Cutler mail-chute boxes roiled with gleaming eagles and light bounced from an ebony Baby Grand. Modest but stylish, the Mayflower had hosted its share of celebrities, from the originators of Felix the Cat to the Bolshoi Ballet. David suddenly laughed out loud. The hotel had also housed a fabled flea circus, with no end of comic possibilities.

"Fleas?" he teased Skidboot, who was oddly free of them, as well as most other canine afflictions, whether parasites, mange or ringworm. The dog either had good genes or good luck.

The hotel's main recommendation was the fabulous location near Times Square and Broadway, one step from the shops, one twirl from the clubs, restaurants and night life. Slightly dowdy, but for the cowboy and his dog, the tightly pulled sheets—so taut they could trampoline in place without even making a dent, at least for a few minutes—was heaven.

"Comfortable," "unpretentious," "your own little secret" described the Mayflower, and David knew that he would add a few more by the time they had finished. One being, "the place where he met his downfall and wished it hadn't happened."

And room service!

"Skidboot, buddy, we are *not* in Texas right now." David strode up and down the room, taking in the two beds and the rainbow play of neon lights from the marquee across the street. Skidboot, watching television, let out a whine.

David brightened up. "You hungry? Well, me too. Let's order."

And when the silver platter arrived, steaming with steak, whipped potatoes, sour cream, butter, Crab Louis salad and a fairyland of tiny appetizers, he nearly collapsed laughing. Carrots fanned out in thin coins, layered with caviar, mushrooms and what looked like chocolate twigs. Patties of some meat substance had been molded into chic torpedoes. And a tiny army of tea sandwiches—he could swear one of them had on an eggwhite cowboy hat—looked like Christmas.

Skidboot bounced and quivered but minded his manners. David relaxed into the lap of contentment, his cares vanished. How quickly luxury took hold.

The Reception people, trendy and urbane, showered them with compliments and then, almost shyly, asked for a few dog tricks. David figured this would help Skidboot work off the effects of a 7-hour flight, and readily obliged. People—rumpled travelers, pancake-faced matrons, Goth entertainers, men with green nails, women with green hair, angelic young things bopping to private music, business travelers—all passed through the old Beaux Arts lobby, perching for a moment on the slightly-worn sofas, eager to see a cowdog do tricks in New York.

As Skidboot rolled, fetched, shadowed and picked up trash, David reviewed the upcoming performance, trying not to panic at the hectoring thought of being in the Ed Sullivan Theater. The venerable 13-story brick building was originally built by Arthur Hammerstein, who named the theater in honor of his father, Oscar. After that, it plunged into troubled times, financial downfall, and numerous name changes until 1935, when CBS began using it for radio broadcasts. Fifteen years later, it became CBS-TV Studio 50, and the home of the Ed Sullivan variety show. In 1993 David Letterman joined CBS, bought the theater and redesigned the space to hold a 400-seat audience. Here the Beatles had performed, and even Elvis had strutted onstage. The celebrity list read like an old issue of *Rolling Stone*—the Doors, Jackson 5, the Mamas and the Papas.

And now, Skidboot and David Hartwig.

It was enough. The specialness David had always felt inside, the knowing of his gifts, all of it had come together here.

CHAPTER FORTY-FOUR

No Applause Sign Needed

By noon they were at the theater, through the Green Room and into the make-up area. Impossibly artistic people glided up to them, offering drinks, taking sound checks. "Skidboot, feels like we're at NASA getting ready for liftoff!" Skidboot nodded, and David stifled a laugh, wondering what kind of make-up a dog might need.

Backstage. Pets and owners cast suspicious glances. Feathers drifted from a rare pygmy parrot that snapped its beak in 2/4 time and rolled its eyes nearly backwards. A python draped casually over the sofa back, but they noticed that its owner always kept her thumb and forefinger pressed hard under the python's chin. None spoke, only pulled their pets close.

David, a notorious icebreaker, noted an older woman clutching a pet pig, her skin tight as her pig's. David leaned across and whispered that he, personally, didn't think it was very nice what people were saying about her dog, *ha ha.*

"What?" She jumped. "Excuse me?

David grinned—that long, drawn-out smirk that presaged comedy and that boosted him right onto the brink of cachinnation.

"Ma'am, when that hair grows back, I'm sure that dog will look as pretty as ever!"

Wide-eyed, she swept her pig into protective custody, where it nuzzled into her bosom and peered out at David. She staggered up out of her seat and swept over to the other side of the waiting room, looking alarmed. David grabbed Skidboot's scruff and sat quietly, waiting to be called.

If life is just a series of firsts, thought David, then this is really living. He'd never been this frightened before. So much fear that it felt catastrophic. He might choke! Skidboot could go rogue. Anything could happen. Then he began to talk himself down. No, this was *playtime.* He and Skidboot were having fun!.

The producer came into the Green Room to deliver last minute instructions. "Ok folks, once Mr. Letterman announces your name, you'll follow me through that curtain. He'll greet you, ask a couple of questions, and then you'll show the audience what your pets can do."

Simple enough. David shuddered, his nerves jumping.

Through the curtain they heard the announcer welcoming the viewing audience to *The Late Show*, mumble, mumble...

"And our next star hails from Quinlan, Texas. Folks, let's welcome David Hartwig and Skidboot. Vivid red applause, lights flashed aggressively overhead and the audience responded by clapping and yelling wildly. *I ought to get me one of them for around the house,* David thought. Things might go a little better.

David Letterman, like Oz, stood at the middle of his vast, bustling, television kingdom, his face genial, bent forward to hear the hoarse response, the failed answer. His glasses glinted, he smiled benevolently. He was here to entertain, not humiliate. Kindly, he asked David what he was about to do.

David's rodeo years slid into effect as he began joking, easily managing the moment right into the game of copycat.

"Copycat?" Skidboot barked impatiently.

"Cat? You don't like that word? Well Mister, there's no such thing as copydog, so we're just going to have to go with it."

Laughter, applause. Skidboot shook his head a few times, then got over it.

And then they began. As focused as a surgical team, David moved and Skidboot mimicked. One boot forward, one paw forward. One step back, one paw back. Hand up, paw up, hand down, paw down. David threw his long length down on the carpet and rolled over, then hopped to his feet nearly stepping on Skidboot, who had thrown himself down, like a soldier navigating a minefield, and was also just hopping up. The drummer rolled out a cadence with each movement and quickly, the audience began to clap.

The crowd was ahead of the 'applause' sign and roared out approval. The applause light begged them to laugh, but everyone was already up and clapping.

David knelt down to Skidboot's ear and whispered, "you done it, boy, you done it."

CHAPTER FORTY-FIVE

The Phantom of the Mayflower

After the show, David and Skidboot relaxed in the lobby, trying to settle down. As usual, people flocked around, eager to see the man in the boots and the dog in the dark glasses. David had succumbed to show business glitz, and bought Skidboot a hat and shades, *just for fun*. He hoped to snap some celebrity photos of themselves in the limo, out of the limo, getting served by waiters — to show Barbara how it was going.

Barbara. David had a slight pang. He sure was having a great time, he wished that she could be there. He tried to call the home number, but no answer.

Then came the hit. The shark circled at first, a well-dressed one, with polished shoes and a narrow cut shirt, slightly unbuttoned, GQ style. All he lacked was a cane, a valet and background music to plunge them into a noir flick.

"Mr. Hartwig?" David couldn't deny it.

"Skidboot?" The query sent Skidboot's back into an angry ruckle, followed by a low snarl.

"Skidboot, you behave now!" The Blue Heeler seldom took dislike to anyone. He expected any new face to be a new fan, but he was having a reaction.

David collared Skidboot, holding him in.

"Jerry Schwartz here." His hand was still outstretched. David managed to shake it but kept a firm grip on Skidboot. "I'm a movie producer, and I have to tell you, I've seen you two perform now a couple of times, and what you have is puuuuuure gold."

David smiled. It never hurt to be showered with praise, and Jerry was a rainmaker of the first order. One velvety blandishment after another. "Dogs like this..." "a rare event..." "something that the film world would..." "never seen anything like it..."

David finally had to stop him. "Mr. Schwartz, let's sit down a minute." The man obliged, lowering himself deeply into a velvet chair where he reclined in a slightly serpentine way, drawing into himself like a man who didn't get much exercise.

He waxed and waned. He vociferated and palavered. He spun out Hollywood success stories as if he was George Lucas. On he went, with much to say because he'd been thinking about it for such a long time. In buttery tones he explained the need for an entire series of Skidboot videos, a Disney-type event, real wholesome. Why, did David know the number of dog owners in the US? The number of people who owned pets? There were pet expos, dog restaurants, even dog matrimonials! There was even talk of a Puppy Channel. Why, with the world as harsh as it was, people needed to enter the world of the dog, to see things in a simple and open hearted way...

"So, what do you need, Mr. Schwartz?" David, used to the handshake agreements of the rodeo circuit, was getting restless with the schmoozing. They'd been at it for nearly an hour, and all he could understand was the repeated "win-win." Jerry would make the videos, Skidboot and David would of course perform, and....

"Well, who pays for this?" David leaned forward. He thought he saw Schwartz flinch.

"We got us a foolproof money raising scheme. Foolproof! It's worked before, it will work again."

Later, David would kick himself for not seeking proof. Which movies had he made? Who had funded them? Where was the paperwork? Then he heard the words, "just sign here and we'll be on our way." Maybe it was New York, or the euphoria of room service, future bookings, private escorts, limos — whatever — that brought the pen into his hand, and after which, he found himself signing, and then heard with perfect clarity: "All we need to do now is to raise the money. And we're on our way!"

Money? David wondered.

What money?

CHAPTER FORTY-SIX

The Hollywood Fiasco

Success had turned into a gravitational field. Wherever they went, it pulled them along, snapping them up short like a rubber band then stretching them out into the future. No sooner home than Art Chapman of the *Ft. Worth Star Times* called up with something about the "Mayflower hotel."

"Beg pardon?" David couldn't quite make it out, but it seemed that someone in the lobby, an oil man from Houston in town to make a drilling deal, had caught their impromptu act in the lobby and called the newspaper. David's celebrity pulled around them like a blanket. *And yes, of course, sir, come on out to the ranch and meet Skidboot.*

When Chapman arrived, he found a ranching family in the middle of a transition, moving from their usual daily chores into the heady chaos of publicity, appointments, trick rehearsal and training. He spent the day photographing, interviewing, and in the end, published a feature story so detailed, so colorful and so moving that Skidboot's rise to stardom was picked up by the wire services, which shot the information to newspapers all over the country.

"What now?" Barbara wondered, her voice nearly drowned out by the ringing of the phone.

"Someone called from the Crook & Chase Talk Show," David yelled back.

"Telephone!" she announced for the fifth time that day. The phone just kept ringing.

"In-cred-i-ble! It's *Inside Edition,* that TV magazine show."

They stared at each other. Keeping an appointment book was falling short. What they needed was a wall-sized blackboard, a flow chart, maybe a retired air traffic controller. Everything felt crazy, lopsided, nearly teetering out of control. Like Jack and the beanstalk, celebrity shot them up into the clouds, exploding new tendrils around them, pushing them ahead of it whether they wanted to go or not.

Skidboot stories spread internationally, bringing a Japanese production company out to the ranch. Dogs in Japan, coddled as children, are dressed up, paraded, fed special dishes, and generally infantilized and idealized. The producers wanted to introduce a new concept, a dog belonging to a "crazy cowboy." But their real agenda was to break Skidboot's concentration using any means available.

They scurried around the ranch, filming David in the saddle, David riding away, leaving Skidboot poised over a toy, far back on the road, quietly waiting for the release number, "three!"

"They keep calling you Ski-boot," David remarked, and Skidboot shrugged. The TV crew kept up their routine until afternoon, when they went to the back room for the final test. The producers cried, "*Ski-boot* will go crazy and bite!" as they tempted him with a bright red plastic truck filled with sushi. Skidboot held his position, never even glancing at this oddity weaving back and forth and smelling weirdly of fish. Tiring of this, they poured tennis balls on the floor, hoping "Ski Boot" would break gaze and attack. Finally, they unleashed a fat Dachshund, which wiggled like a live hot dog across the floor but provoked only *more* disinterest. Finally, they sighed, conferred, called everyone "crazy," packed up and left.

Everything takes its toll, and in their case, Barbara worried that Skidboot was overworked. "He can't be on all the time, David. He needs to play, to just to be a dog."

"You're like a stage mother," David tried to joke. But it was true. Their family life was skewed. The idea of all of them gathered around the TV, eating popcorn, laughing and relaxing, seemed a thing of the past, and sometimes, no one could remember whether it was even a true memory or not.

Wistfully, Barbara mentioned going to a movie. "How about tonight?"

David grew still. A movie? Weren't they going to be *in* a movie? That seemed to take precedence over just *going* to a movie, and he reminded her that the movie producer, Schwartz, was due over the next day. She stared at the floor, alone with her thoughts, while David herded Skidboot out to the truck.

"Come on, copilot!" David laughed, hopped in and opened Skidboot's door. That stopped him for a minute, thinking. Why, the dog had been shotgun in this truck more than his wife! Or Russell. But then, Russell's studies kept him in Dallas. He shrugged it off.

They sat in the front seat and both felt that prickle of excitement when a trick was about to take place, almost a kind of ground charge.

Skidboot stared intently at the ignition, nearly trembling.

"Ok, ok," David put in the key.

Skidboot stared at the gearshift, again, nearly trembling.

"Ok, ok,? David shifted to drive.

Skidboot, now on four feet standing on the seat, touched his nose to the wheel.

"Ok, ok, we'll go." But Skidboot was still frozen near the wheel, pointing.

"What, you want to drive?" Skidboot yapped, a quick one for "yes."

"Well, pal, that's one thing you can't do, at least not on public roads." With that, the truck roared to life and jumped away from the curb.

Barbara retreated back into the mobile home, shuffled furniture around, dusted a little and washed some dishes. Suddenly, she jumped. Someone had shouted "David Hartwig" loud, right in the study. With no one there, she had a moment's unease before she realized it was the radio. Then she heard David, in a low drawl, telling the story of Skidboot to anyone tuned in to nighttime radio. Must be some kind of religious program,

Barbara thought. Not religious herself, she shied away from programs like this. She heard some preacher — she strained to hear the name — making a mighty thin comparison between discipleship, a man and his dog.

She swept over to the radio.

"A special word found in discipleship is disciple!" The preacher droned on.

Okay, she thought.

"That's what God wants for us all! And before we can disciple, we must learn discipline. Without one, God can't have the other. And right here in Quinlan, Texas, we have a manifestation of His work. Right here with David Hartwig and his dog." Deep, oratorical tones, revival style, bore the name "Hartwig" out to a thousand listeners. When the preacher said "his dog," Barbara tried not to sulk, but the slights and oversights just kept mounting. David might be the trainer, but Skidboot was HER dog!

CHAPTER FORTY-SEVEN

Film Financing?

Life out of balance will inevitably self-correct. It happens in Nature, it happens in history, and it especially happens in Greek tragedies. Even in modern American drama, the struggles of the common turn tragic, although the better word might be "poorly." Heroic struggles involve heroes, and David, despite his sense of being an exception, was still a rancher and a cowboy. And today, he had a strange, sinking feeling, as if something astonishing was going to happen.

And it did.

That night was the neighborhood round-up, the night that Jerry Schwartz, the movie producer, had nagged him about for the past month. "Get your friends together as investors, David. Give your buddies a place on the bandwagon."

Barbara had met the man, and had one word: "creepy."

"Why so, Barbara?" David kept trying to make things right with everyone, and here was a chance to promote Skidboot. No, actually, it was a chance to honor Skidboot, as well as help out all the friends who had helped him over the years. If anything was win-win, this was it.

"There's just something about him."

Of course there was, David pointed out. The guy produces movies. He breathes, sleeps, looks and acts Hollywood, and even in Texas, people should understand what that means. Hollywood meant money, bent values and a craving for novelty — its alien aura just flowed off Jerry. But then, if he were just a humdrum guy, steady as a bank teller, he'd hardly be out there producing movies, would he?

They were thrown into the odd dilemma of believing that distrust might equal success, while in the deepest places of understanding, they also knew it just wasn't true. But people were arriving. It was their first investor's meeting.

Cars pulled up, doors slammed, headlight beams crisscrossed, then died. The dining room table groaned under the spread — David wanted to treat his friends to a nice repast as well, homemade carrot cake, chips and beer, an ambrosia salad from the Deli, cold cuts and cheese. Surprised, they settled around the table, Richard Banks, Della Cathcar, Howard and Mindy Atkinson and others. More could have come, and maybe would have, if he'd extended it further. But this was a core group, a special group. David glanced over at his parents and met his father's direct gaze.

I trust you, the glance said.

David felt a pang. This was a man on a pension. *What if....?* He refused to think about it. He had to stay positive. Thanks to Skidboot, David had a chance to *give back.* The golden moment shimmered, invited. It was a supercharged and miraculous moment, like so many others this past year.

"Thank you all for attending this investor meeting," Schwartz began. They noted the man, his basic otherness. Everyone here wore jeans, but his jeans looked iridescent, and hung differently. The men all wore belts, some glinting with championship roping buckles, but Jerry's belt, flat and silver studded, seemed faintly Navajo. Here the men wore western work shirts, narrow cut, pearl buttoned, fit for the saddle, while his eggplant dark shirt, casually unbuttoned, two down, shouted "film director."

"And so I'm a film director..." he continued, tracing out the path of his many credits, dropping names, striding back and forth, which made everyone nearly dizzy trying to follow the gist.

But the gist, clearly, was investor output, meaning money. The money to finance a Hollywood movie about Skidboot, a movie that would touch hearts everywhere, rival Disney for family appeal, tap into a national psyche that had never, really, gotten over the *real* Rin Tin Tin, the *real* Lassie, and provide the perfect sequel. Schwartz spun out his vision, his voice soothing, while people glanced down at their hands, embarrassed. This never happened in Quinlan, except maybe for Mary Kay house parties. Seldom was there the public drumming up of money, the promise of rewards. Simple folk, country people — they watched Barbara and David to gauge their reactions.

David looked serious, nodding in agreement. Barbara had gotten up to make another pot of coffee but stayed there for a surprisingly long time.

By evening's end, everyone had pledged an amount, each to the ability to give, but all persuaded that this homegrown miracle—Skidboot and the Hartwigs—deserved their support. For many, this was as close as they would come to a speculative investment. Few of them even had stock accounts. Although the individual donations were modest, for everyone that night, it felt enormous.

CHAPTER FORTY-EIGHT

Skidboot Meets Oprah

Barbara opened a groggy eye. Light filtered in, suffusing the room in a pale hue. She had a moment's confusion because outside she heard the sound of David yelling, "What on earth...?" Usually she was up first, ready with coffee. But after last night she'd slept in.

Throwing her robe around her, she peered out the front door.

David, hands on hips, was lecturing Skidboot, who sat obediently, head cocked to the side, bright eyes unblinking.

"...and you know this is a new truck, and you know that you DO NOT jump up on this door here and leave scratch marks."

"David!" She didn't like the way things had been going. One minute, the dog was their teenager, someone to instruct, hang out with, make plans with. The next minute, he was a bad dog, getting disciplined.

"Give him a break. He's worked enough! Let him play."

David shrugged, muttered. And she heard, "that dog's gonna make us money at the *Pet Star* finale. You can't have it both ways."

She knew that. Her Skidboot, that cuddly Heeler she loved to slip snacks to, who waited in the dirt outside the corral for the sound of her truck, who panted for her like no one else and who now earned more than she and David did together. Confusion welled up, but thrilled her, too. Who wouldn't be excited?

And that truck! Shiny as an ice palace. Why, it had such high gloss she wondered if there might be a safety issue for oncoming traffic.

She couldn't resist pointing out how nice the truck was, glamorous, really. In fact, a truck like that would just about pay for the roof they so desperately needed.

Silence.

David shrugged, trying to be patient. "Honey, we are gonna get a new roof for sure. It just won't be the kind you're thinking of."

She frowned. Now, what did that mean?

And as surely as the sun sets, she found out.

David squealed out of the driveway right after their discussion. He felt empowered—the movie, ongoing prize money that pumped their bank account up above "flush" into record new zones. Heaven had opened up, spilling blessings down on them, so many that they spattered around, overflowed. One of the things David had learned in his life with animals—being a "whisperer" type—was to tune into the fine vibrations of meaning. *You might not understand, but you never walk away.*

And this theory brought him to the finance office of a mobile home dealer in downtown Quinlan, situated in a maze of tidy offices and behemoth double-wides, parked tight as tuna, just waiting to be paid for and driven away. Some were up to 3,000 square feet, true luxury living. He'd made the call simply in the spirit of inquiry, thinking that he and Barbara could talk it over when he got the details. From past failures in the credit world, David didn't have high hopes. But it never hurt to try.

So he leaned across the shiny laminate table to squint at the figures that Elm Baker, the finance manager, had compiled. His eyes blurred when he heard the words "credit score a little low..." Well. *Tell me something new...*

David settled back, sighing. Then he made to rise, held out his hand.

"Now wait a minute, David," Elm grew moist and inviting, his big brow gleaming with presale shine. Wouldn't do to let a hot one get away, even if the score was low.

"All that means is we can't get you top-tier financing, but with a $10,000 down payment, we can swing you $60,000 at 16%." David heard him through a blur of excitement...$10,000? *Why, Skidboot could cough that up the next time the phone rang!*

Before he knew it, out flew his checkbook, out came his pen and zeroes were looping along the money line of the check like a counterfeiter.

Every man—and woman—deserves the luxury of writing a big check sometime in life, and this was David's moment.

"You'll hold onto this for three days, as per the agreement?" He wanted to be sure, as if viewing the new mobile home wasn't enough. Unsaid, of course, was the most important item: what would Barbara say?

"Skidboot," he instructed, you go take a look. Skidboot calmly walked around the mobile home, sniffing, arching his back, ears thrust forward to scoop up any new information, nose sniffing like a wild thing, but knowing that he should *not* pee to mark turf. The idea that his family—his family!—would have this shiny new device, not unlike the other shiny new device, the truck— felt good. All Skidboot wanted was what David wanted, a chance to grapple together, come up with new tricks, outwit each other and now, have a shiny huge new home on wheels. What more could a dog ask?

Well, one thing. That his real owner, Barbara, would be as happy as he was. And right now, as Skidboot nestled at her feet, basking in the hot beam of the overhead table light, companionably munching hanger steak and Ora-Ida fries just sizzled out of the frying pan, he felt contentment swirl around him, cloudlike, soothing, working its domestic spell. He knew they only had a little time until the airport. Then he and David would fly somewhere, again. But for now, the peace welled up.

A bolt of energy shot through him as Barbara jumped up, pushed her plate away and gripped the edge of the table. Skidboot flopped backwards. He winced as her voice staggered up an octave.

"You what?"

Skidboot couldn't help them out, not now. He cowered under the table, nose pressed tight between his paws as the words flew back and forth, "bad decision," "we don't have that kind of money," "get the check back!" and so on. David stood unfazed. He had grabbed the chance to give his family a better home, one without a sagging roof, rusting pipes and mystery stains. One they could be proud of, something new. They were part of a new world now, where fundraising set the pace. You raised funds for movies. You raised funds for new mobile homes. Same thing, just a different kind of world than the one they knew. After all, he and Skidboot had been on Jay Leno and Letterman. How big was that?

Didn't Barbara understand that their circle had widened? That he had to gallop to keep up with circumstances, take advantage of the momentum? Within hours they would be on Oprah. The thought was stunning.

"Barbara, you know we have to get to the airport. You going to take us?"

And with the knifelike precision of a surgeon chopping away flesh, the strokes were made. No, she would not take them. And no, don't even ask about picking them up. Words, sharp and bitter, hung in the air. David grabbed the phone, called a taxi, and with extra vehemence, said;

"I need a cab to Dallas/Ft. Worth. I'm out here in Quinlan on Shady Trail. Look for the rusted old trailer with the torn roof. You can't miss it. I'll be waiting outside."

That valuable newlywed canon, "never let the sun set on your anger," was broken. The sun set, then rose, and the raw bitter feelings hung between them. If there was guilt, it had to do with the fact that right now, at the zenith of the family's career, in the week when David would appear on Oprah, Barbara would choose not to watch. Or, if she did, it would be a brief flick, just to see how her dog was doing.

Because she never went on the trips, she didn't see that Skidboot now had his own first class seat—*first class!* That David had slipped Hollywood shades down on Skidboot's nose, matching the exact pair that he also wore, in fact, the pair that he had dreamed about. And that the two of them cut quite a sight as they sipped cocktails and ate chocolates. Skidboot particularly liked truffles, and with luck and time, David might even get him to bark out something that sounded like *trrr-rrr-ufff-fffle!* Or not.

Now this was living! Skidboot had graduated to the plane's first class, almost personhood status. He couldn't wait to see what was next in store.

CHAPTER FORTY-NINE

A Star Is Born

What would it be like to always live like this, being served little shrimp cakes with curled fronds of green onion sticking out like stalks? David mused, staring out the window.

"Sir, I saw you two last night..." The stewardess smiled at them, handing David an extra set of cocktail nuts. He told her about their next gig, the Oprah Show.

"Oprah!" Thrilled, she told two of the other stewardesses, and he could see them buzzing up front. It was happening so fast that his head couldn't keep up.

Plus, he'd never seen Chicago before. It was hard for him to tell what he liked more, the idea of holing up in a fancy hotel, enjoying amenities, watching TV, soaking in the tub, looking out over the sparkling lights of a huge urban metropolis and realizing, that out there, all those lights belonged to people who would soon be watching him. It was dazzling.

Celebrity spun its own web, attracting people on the street, lending the patina of glamour to the duo from Texas. When people saw the pointy boots, the slouch Stetson, the dog with the kerchief, they stared, or followed, or more often, recognized them. "Skidboot!

Look, it's Skidboot!" followed them as they strolled down Michigan Avenue in the coldest, windiest city in America. Astonishingly, people asked them for autographs and photos. Luckily, David had a full stock of black and white glossies, and each one he gave out came with a short bark from Skidboot.

"He's saying, 'thank you very much,'" David translated, and people would clap and squeal. By the time they finally appeared on Oprah, David felt surrounded by a magical presence, a comforting web of practiced response. Oprah, herself, also made them comfortable. If David were to think about it at length, the phenomenon of Oprah, like that of Skidboot, seemed without precedent. What brought a person, or a dog, out of obscurity into the eyes of the world? Oprah began her broadcasting career at WVOL radio in Nashville while still in high school. At 19, she was the youngest, as well as the first African-American woman news anchor at Nashville's WTVF-TV. Then her career took off; she co-anchored, then turned co-host to a local talk show. A Chicago morning talk show was next, then national syndication, then her own Harpo Studios. Her career continued to explode, shooting her to the number one talk show slot for twenty four consecutive seasons, inspiring and delighting more than 40 million viewers weekly in the United States, as well as being licensed to 150 countries internationally.

Soon after came OWN, the Oprah Winfrey Network, followed by a magazine and newsletter subscribers.

Oprah's career was simply...exponential. It multiplied on a quantum basis, a human interest zephyr flying out of bounds. Despite her sophistication, grace and spiraling success, at times the wide-eyed girl in pigtails appeared, and in her earnest expression David read something familiar: a desire to entertain, to share the joy, to give happiness.

Skidboot sensed her warmth and fluttered his eyes at her just before plunging into the Beeping Trick. By now he could find a phone if it was in the next county, so darting into fake stage foliage, burrowing around, and pulling out a cordless phone was child's play. If there was any wrong move on the show, it happened when David told Oprah that Skidboot was the most important thing in the world to him. Show business talk, quickly forgotten. The subject changed so fast he had no chance to thank Barbara, to make the usual kudos and caveats to his beloved family members.

But Barbara heard, and her eyes narrowed. Of course, she knew what he meant, but she stood up with a swift motion and turned off the show. Lately, she'd spent a lot of time turning things off.

CHAPTER FIFTY

A Price for Everything

Another phone call, this time from a casting director who wondered if Skidboot could travel to Dallas for an audition.

"A movie?" David asked, still bemused by the idea of stardom. But this one was different because Skidboot might be in it, not the subject of it. And it's Dallas location meant an easy trip, only 27 miles away.

"Sure," David agreed, never one to turn down an adventure. When they arrived at the casting offices, once again he felt the hot breeze of film success, a heady mixture of anticipation, bright lights and glowing reviews. Heady stuff for a cowboy and his dog, and David, when asked if Skidboot would work with someone else, made a quick commitment: "Sure, just tell him what to do."

The director, a thin man in floppy pants, his face darkened like a pirate by a stylish 5'o clock shadow, beckoned the dog.

"Skidboot, get in your place." Amazingly, without any idea of where that was, Skidboot found it and settled there, never casting a look at David for support or instruction. David felt a flash of disappointment, *could his dog switch over so easily?*

"Skidboot, copy me." The director walked and Skidboot walked behind him, as if aware that every move he made took him closer to being...a star!

"Skidboot, now let's roll." Again, without any preview of words, intent or behavior, when the director fell to his belly, Skidboot sank down too. "Hmmm," the director cocked an eyebrow, considering. Then he asked David if they could stay a minute while everyone took a second look. Stage hands trooped by, making crooning infantile sounds. *Why do people use baby talk to animals?* David wondered. *They aren't babies.* Light screens and cameras rotated, moved in close, then receded in a buzz and whine of electricity.

Who else was auditioning? There might be Mastiffs, Shar-pei's, French Bulldogs with shovel shaped faces.

"Could you get him to move back 3-feet?" David motioned to Skidboot, *move back 3-feet,* and he jumped back so quickly that clipboards dropped, and a buzz erupted, with Skidboot's name repeated, followed by "look at that!" David wondered about the next segment, when Skidboot had to steal a valise from a salesman, nose it open and fling the papers around.

Perfect. They'd written this role for Skidboot.

Within seconds, Skidboot had translated "valise," remembered the word "steal" and reverted back to his puppyhood, growling, gnawing and raging around in circles as he shook the valise empty, its tornado of papers caught up in the roar of a wind machine. David worried that the huge exhaust might spook Skidboot but saw that it only revved him up.

"He has *so* got this role!" they cried, and the weeks that ensued finally culminated in the Hartwigs — Barbara and David, dressed in tux and satin — at the premier. They'd thought about a dog tux for Skidboot but left him home. This would be date night for the Quinlan couple, a time to bask in the glow.

CHAPTER FIFTY-ONE

Declined

The new leather sofa gleamed in the light, buttery and soft. It was a showroom sofa, a CEO's kind of sofa, the sort that pulled you into an opulent embrace and wouldn't let you go. Which, at the moment, was exactly David's intent as he lounged there, straddled in comfort, inhaling the clean, brown leather essence, like a new baseball glove. In front of him was the flashy, new, big screen TV amid the flowers that Barbara had clustered on the table, chrysanthemums in a burst of fall colors. Sometimes, contentment seemed almost palpable. Everything was in place.

He ran a quick review:

Russell. Law school, excellent grades. Check.

Skidboot. Nearly 3-years of entertaining and he just got smarter. Check.

David. More at ease daily and looking forward to making a movie. Check.

Barbara. Well. Hmmm. He couldn't quite check her off, which made him feel sad.

Dinner always pulled them together. Skidboot, now with his own chair and place setting, looked like some kid in a Halloween costume. "Hey, elbows off the table!" David yelled, and Skidboot jumped. Then he slid them — his elbows! — down below the table line. David thought about other dogs, then wondered whether a dog even *had* elbows. Other dogs from Quinlan led *unstructured* lives. One ate a $20 bill. Another stole bacon off the table. A third polished off the fall decorations at the Oktoberfest, dried leaves and all. And here was Skidboot, weaned long ago from misbehaving, a dog who exercised control at all times, banished illogic, craziness, or any behavior that didn't make sense. *Did he ever miss his doggie days of simple, stupid fun?*

Oh well. David balanced the phone to his ear while he passed the roast beef, tidily cutting off a juicy strip for Skidboot.

"More gigs," he announced, letting Barbara know how the day had gone.

Barbara nodded, *uh-huh* and then looked away. Skidboot whined, looking from one to the other. What's wrong here? He could frown better than any human, pulling his mottled blue eyebrows down into a grumpy ruckle along his nose, which then made him sneeze. Then his shoulders shook.

He looked back and forth at his people. He could remember the past. He knew that he doted on Barbara, his first person. Remember the fun?

He whined, thinking back to the State Fair. He and David got bored quickly with the same routine, so one day David borrowed a smock and a broom from one of the sweep-up guys, then Barbara rode her horse out into the arena, leading a second horse. Skidboot had trembled with excitement—he had no idea what was about to happen!

One of David's best ideas was to mix things up, surprise Skidboot with a new trick, improvise. The idea was to keep him alert.

Alert? Skidboot ate alert for breakfast! He was perpetually alert. But David believed that if he changed commands, invented new tricks—like this one—that Skidboot would have to listen, intuit and sharpen up his reasoning skills.

So Barbara flounced her pretty hair and sat straight in the saddle and announced, well, bragged, really, about what her horse could do. On and on she went, the horse reigned tight and semi-prancing, but meanwhile...

David, wearing the custodial white, followed by Skidboot, began sweeping up around the arena. While Barbara went on, David commanded Skidboot, "over there, pick up please," and Skidboot would trot over, pick up a paper cup and throw it in the trash.

After several distracting minutes, Barbara cried out, "Sir! You and your dog are interrupting my program!"

"Oh, so sorry, ma'am." David apologized.

Minutes later in the middle of her spiel, Skidboot retrieved a Sprite can, trotted it over to the trash, stood up on his hind legs and threw it in.

"Sir!" she said again...

"Oh, sorry about that...."

By now, the crowd was laughing, full out. They knew this had turned into a routine, and they loved the snappy way the dog went back and forth with the trash, while Barbara, buzzed as a bee, finally said, "Sir! if you can't clear the arena, at least you can help me ride this extra horse! I need someone to ride the fresh off of him."

Skidboot loved this memory. David had agreed, and told Skidboot to go over and get that horse, and Skidboot *did* go get the horse, delicately taking the reins from Barbara's hands, leading the horse over to David, who jumped astride. The horse duo slowly turned to the right, and Skidboot imitated them. Then the horses turned left, went ten feet, and backed up. Skidboot did the same thing. By now, a musician had struck up, "Don't Fence Me In" while the three of them moved around the arena, trailing laughter and applause.

I loved that! Skidboot scratched delicately behind one ear, remembering how they all worked together, man, woman, and dog—a real team.

A sigh went out, but whose? All three at the table now had regrets. In fact...

"Brrrrrrr!" The doorbell rang.

The mood broke. David leaped up, opened it to find Art Shipley. Shame flooded over him, remembering the last time when his neighbor had dangled the dead chicken, Skidboot's kill.

"Art? Not again?"

Art laughed easily, pushing his hat back, stepping into the room. He took in the dinner scene and promised he'd scoot and let them finish, only he had this one thing....

"Got me a female heeler in heat, David. I'd like to pay you to have Skidboot sire."

Instant relief. David realized that no, this wasn't a complaint call, in fact, it was a chance to earn a good piece of change. With Skidboot's genes, Art could pump up top prices for his litter. It made good business sense. Only, it would never be.

"Art, the best I can do is run down one of his siblings."

Surprise etched his friend's face. Was David playing coy with his dog?

"I can pay $1,000 and give you the pick of the litter." Art looked confused until David explained what few people knew, that Skidboot had been fixed and would never father pups. Skidboot, true to form, was the only one of his kind.

Art looked embarrassed, glanced quickly over at Skidboot, as if to see how he felt about it. Finding only the usual perky look, he told David that, well, that might be okay for him, but that he, Art, knew a champion when he saw it, and he was going to find the rest of the family, and pronto.

No problem, they agreed. It was a good deal, one to grasp hands and shake on. After Art left, the phone rang again, this time Russell, who had decided to join the army after graduation.

"Really?" Pride spilled over. They smiled, content with the idea but also with the fact that he would have to graduate first, and a lot could happen between graduation from SMU and basic training.

Minutes later, another shrill interruption. This time, Quinlan Elementary wanted to know if he and Skidboot could come entertain the children?

Still swayed by the events of the past months, a medley of easy money and even easier work that seemed to flow his way, he blurted out, "how much?"

The shock on Barbara's face stopped him.

"How much?" She was incredulous.

By now pride had taken over. He'd made the statement, he was in the business of keeping them going, and being in business meant charging for services rendered, even if it was a school.

"That's right. How much. And be sure and let me know."

CHAPTER FIFTY-TWO

Embezzled and Embarrassed

Packed and ready to leave for home, David looked back on the last performance with pride, yet another big city success, one in a long string of them, as he blithely handed his credit card to the front desk clerk. Sometimes he couldn't believe how comfortable he'd gotten with travel and all its amenities, like being a member of a private, airborne club. And this hotel had entranced him, with the nearly walk-in television, handy room service, and the skyline of Manhattan shimmering outside his window. Even the Visa card recently linked to the new Skidboot account, replete of funds taken in for the movie, filled him with a sense of deep satisfaction. The center held, the world felt stable, everything was golden.

"I'm sorry sir, your card was declined."

Declined? "Run it again, please." *They always make mistakes...*

The clerk's knowing expression said that he'd heard it all before, and adjusting his wire-frame glasses, he tapped his fingers as they both waited for the distant gods of credit to spit forth a new and better decision.

"Sorry sir, declined again. Do you have another form of payment?"

Declined. What a terrible word. Sick people declined. To be declined was to be deselected, no longer part of operative society. He'd spent months being solvent, now he hardly knew what to do. But worse, where was the money....?

Luckily, his wallet was stuffed with "emergency" funds, the sum total of a three-night stay. How he'd kept that much cash free, he didn't know, but thanked Divine Providence. Meanwhile, he and his Blue Heeler were walking the streets of Manhattan with just enough for cab fare to the airport. Luckily, he had a plane ticket....and a few extra dollars for an emergency. Again, he tried to reach Barbara, but the phone hammered into silence, then clicked onto her voice mail and its patient automated response. Finally, he remembered that he could call the bank and plug into the account menu, so he waited, toes tapping the pavement, as the menu clicked through various options, finally landing him in the auto summation of the account balance—an astounding amount of *negative* forty dollars and thirty four cents.

Negative?

Sucker punched, the breath flew out of him. He leaned against a wall, shivering. Only Jerry Schwartz had access to the account. No one else did, other than David and Barbara.

He called and left Barbara another message, this one pleading, begging her to call back, telling her to check the business account. "Something's wrong!"

The Times building rose up like a rocket ship, and across the street, huge neon signs flashed extravagance, announcing a musical popular in Manhattan, epicenter of the world's entertainment industry. Yet David didn't even have the money for a hot dog, much less a ticket.

Waves of homesickness lapped and wavered, bringing various images to mind, first Barbara, then Russell — where was his boy now? And the ranch...wasn't it time for the annual Quilt Fair? He laughed, knowing that to even think of the quilt fair showed his anxious state — really, quilts? Gathering Skidboot's shorthair neck folds in his hand, he massaged and petted the dog, going down on one knee to get closer, to gather him into his arms, just to be.

It's ok. Skidboot gazed up at him, *It's ok.*

But going home now felt harsh and unwelcoming. He had to contact his contributors, that select club of fellow ranchers and family members who had flirted with Hollywood, each supporting his dream with money, but secretly, drawn to the big lights, the big names, the idea of being one with the stars.

But the real Hollywood moment would come the next week, when they filed into the Hartwig living room, jostling and eager for news, ribbing and joking about show business. David had called the meeting. They grew quiet as he loomed over them.

"Friends, I have some news...."

Of *course* he did! The first million, someone joked. Sure, a million *each*, someone joked back. The buzz rumbled and wavered, then died down. As David bowed his head, he felt as if he was presiding over a funeral, offering regrets over the short, sweet life of the Skidboot project.

"…..and so, that's what happened." His words dragged in the air, bitter as smoke, *cleaned out, money gone.* Like a scene from *The Sting*, they discovered that a thief's machinations knew no bounds when it came to money — *their* money. Someone blinked, a quick wiping of the eyes. Ralph James snorted, then grew quiet. They were once again as they had started, simple folks, friends and family, only lighter in the bankroll, some by many thousands. They talked in low voices, some looking guarded, some even craning around, some seeking signs of high living. They didn't want to, not really, it was just an instinct.

"New truck, David?" The words pierced the air, keen with intent, driving a wedge among friends. The pride David felt in this hard-won purchase — a purchase based only on Skidboot's earnings — suddenly took on malicious meaning. *Did they actually think….?*

Suddenly, Barbara burst out:

"Every one of you knows this man. You know he would die before he'd take a cent that wasn't his. You all will recoup your money if it takes David the rest of his life to repay you."

More murmurs, and David looked gratefully at her. She frowned, because part of the hurt stemmed from Skidboot, too.

"David, " she said, "I am tired of this dog being used only for money."

David hung his head, sheepish and disappointed. Even his parents' encouragement didn't help. "The dog is special, son, and so are you. You all got a story to tell. Why, you two are larger than life right now. Makes sense that your troubles would be extra big, too." Thankful once again for his parents, he remembered how his high school friends wanted to have *his* parents instead of their own, how Pat and Rudy always offered good advice, provided a home without discord.

As they filed out, some stopped to stare at the truck, others at the new trailer. But by the next week, no one was there to see David drive the truck back to the showroom and unceremoniously, with steely determination, trade it down.

CHAPTER FIFTY-THREE

A Turn for the Worse

All good stories need a reversal.

It can happen midway or toward a story's end, it's timing less important than the change it signifies. Afterwards, the pace picks up, and action begins to flow speedily uphill again in the opposite direction.

Sometimes the results are brief. But sometimes, they can last forever.

In David's case, the reversal just kept happening, as if falling through the matrix, or like an Olympic luge racer plunging downhill toward a faraway finish line. And the faster he plunged, the more he began to feel different about things.

For one, the sense of fierce ambition, the steely drive to earn, burn and churn—it lessened. He still ran his dog—his *fixed asset* as well as his best buddy. He loved the attention and wouldn't turn down the income, but somehow, it all felt...*different*.

It might have been that day at Quinlan elementary, when he strode into the class with Skidboot, grumpy and discouraged by the crooked movie deal, by his sense of gloomy responsibility, by the huge, tottering magnitude of what they'd built...it was just getting to him. And the First Grade teacher, her curly hair framing wide glasses, finally relaxed her worried look as she met them and fixed on Skidboot.

"Look, class, he's here!" And the swarm of overalls, scuffed Nikes and runny noses surged up to them, then dallied around the dog, giddy with affection, until Miss Gray, embarrassed, thrust out a glass container filled with coins and crumpled bills.

"Mr. Hartwig, we're so sorry. We were in the middle of collecting your money, and well, you're a little early. We'll get the rest for sure...."

Hot shame, a flood of embarrassment. David felt a tug, as Skidboot pawed him from below. *Are you kidding, David? Look at these children...."*

David tried to shake it all off and proceed with the one-two trick, but Skidboot just sat there, staring at the children, then at the glass jar. It only took a few minutes, but soon they were both staring at the glass jar, as disturbing as if it held a live viper.

"Kids, you take your money back!" David thrust the jar back at the teacher while Skidboot whined happily at his feet. The children watched, wide-eyed. He'd heard of teachable moments and figured that this probably was one, either for him or them. "And so," he said, feeling humble, "this dog does what he does out of love. And you all know that love doesn't have a price."

David, embarrassed, felt like his life had turned into a Hallmark special. He turned to Skidboot. *Satisfied?* Skidboot smiled in that particular way a dog does, his face stretched into a semicircle of approval and excitement, his muzzle and whiskers upswept, followed by a wag, a wriggle, then a long whine as he pawed the floor, as in *let's do it!* Skidboot was ready to commence.

As the day wore on, life opened up, refreshed by the freedom of giving. David was no stranger to generosity —but time and the celebrity jackhammer had left him feeling run down, run over. He shot a quick look at Skidboot as they jutted along the road, heading home, the old truck laboring as they cut through swales of oat hay and blooming switchgrass.

And Skidboot? The same, he himself might say, except that his pointed muzzle now bore flecks of grey, giving a salt and pepper quality that turned his usual blue-black mottle more variegated, dappled as a meadow. A few grey hairs dotted his nape and chest, a light dusting, like sugar. But the vigor remained. An artist drawing Skidboot would start by making a brisk U-shaped curve—tippy nose high on the one side, stiff tail high on the other, and in between, a short-haired coat, tense with excitement.

Skidboot, as tasked as a CEO, needed complex and surprising work, and if either he or David ran out, someone would invent something new. Other dogs might chase blackbirds or steal the breakfast bacon, but Skidboot, caught between man and canine, generally adhered to the lesson David had taught him: *good manners, no matter what,*

As much as they understood each other, David had no way of reading his companion, any more than Skidboot could read himself. Skidboot shunned noise in favor of action and seldom howled, yelped or made a ruckus — until that day.

David was changing the oil on the old Ford, and finishing up, wiped his hands and sprayed himself clean with the hose. Just then, a frantic, high-range howl burst out. Then silence.

"Wha...? Skidboot!" David dropped the Pennzoil and loped up the rise to the field where he'd left the dog only minutes before. A limp form lay on the ground, all life gone from it. He ran forward, yelling. No movement.

Kneeling, he watched a horseshoe-shaped contusion well up around the muzzle and spread down toward his jaw, which hung agape at a strange angle. That familiar smile now drooped open, just as his eyes stayed sealed. A thread of blood seeped onto to the ground. Skidboot had been kicked by a horse.

As they gathered him up, Barbara and David were spinning out of control, trying to understand what had happened. Their dog was fast. What on earth slowed him down to the point of being in the danger zone of a horse? It was unthinkable...Skidboot?

Barbara sobbed, her shoulders hunched as she bent over her dog. David thundered around the trailer looking for the telephone, throwing cushions in the air, finally pressing the locator on the phone base, over and over, until it wailed like a baby from the back room. In seconds he was calling an ambulance, describing the tragedy..."kicked by a horse in the head," "unconscious," "three and a half years old." Then he gave the address.

He looked at the telephone, incredulous.

"No, it's not our son. It's our dog!" He darkened, his drawl unleashed. "You won't WHAT? You can't send an ambulance?"

He threw down the phone. They made a cloth sled out of a beach blanket and carefully rolled Skidboot over onto it. A small moan hung in the air, then trailed off.

"My God," David whispered, picking the dog and the towel up, running to the truck. "Hold on, Skidboot, just hold on."

CHAPTER FIFTY-FOUR

Blind Love

The vet's sympathy usually went first to animals, next to people. But the pair facing him now were in bad shape.

"It's going to be all right," he sympathized. "Your dog was kicked, has a broken jaw and a severe concussion. All these will mend."

He meant to continue, because the relief blew out of them, a mighty exhale, but he had more to tell them.

"There's still a problem..." They waited, the suspense running up and down like the flu. Their hearts twisted when he told them, and suddenly, it all made sense. Skidboot was kicked because he didn't *see* the horse. It appeared dim in his vision, which was progressing rapidly toward a form of blindness, Progressive Retinal Atrophy. "You never noticed...?" made them feel like bad parents, thoughtless owners, forcing their blind dog to perform tricks, like a scene out of Dickens.

They thought back over Skidboot's behavior, and David remembered those few times when Skidboot fumbled his toy, which David had wondered about, briefly, but didn't really think through. Still, how could Skidboot have managed so well?

The diagnosis fell on them, a fatal blow. "No treatment for this condition. A bit of eyesight left , but the good eye will only get worse... ....."

When they gathered Skidboot up to take him home, there was nothing in his dull expression to remind them of the Vaudeville dog, the show dog who sucked up applause, proudly trotted next to his human partners, exuded love to the crowds. As the days passed, Skidboot hung on, but barely, seldom eating, letting out small noises as someone passed by, a sound nearly muffled by the bandages.

Daily, they'd prop him up on the sofa facing the television as David anxiously watched from the other room to see a spark of interest. But Skidboot slumped down, listless and stared toward the window. David thought he might be attracted to animals, so he flipped the channel to *Pet Star*.

"Skidboot," he whispered, "you remember? Look at that." Today's star pig buried her snout in a book, turning the pages slowly by nose. David watched Skidboot to see if the friendly little squeals would perk him up. But no, no interest in pigs.

And even when the doorbell rang and David opened it to see Mel, the postman, wrestling with three stuffed bags of mail, did Skidboot show no interest. "For your poor little dog," Mel sympathized, dropping them at the porch. David dragged them in, spilled out the contents and, incredulous, started to read.

Hearts flew open as children wrote to Skidboot. School classes sent him handmade cards, red construction paper with wobbly drawings. And the faithful folks sent prayers spiraling upwards, invoking his recovery.

"Look at this!" David tried to interest him, and even invented a game of "when I count to *three* then I'll get you another letter." Maybe a dash of the old "three" routine would spark him up a little. But no, Skidboot just stared blankly, eyes dark, unfathoming.

Meanwhile, news stations chanted the litany of his successes, his appearance credits, his tricks, his happy nature, his prognosis. The telephone jangled and buzzed. The plight of the wounded Blue Heeler had touched America, and America, judging from the fat, overstuffed mail sacks, wanted to touch him back. (Years later, bloggers would blog, friends would email each other, U-tube videos would invade Ethernet lines, as an electronic Skidboot tsunami would continue to sweep across the country).

Rest and recuperation, the vet had said. And David and Barbara provided it. For weeks, Skidboot lay there, watching them with his senses, beginning to lap a little milk, then chow, then moving slowly into the room, still limping. They celebrated every advance, and David, somewhat clowning, but really trying to spark Skidboot into excitement, would throw himself on the floor and go into a routine, rolling around, inviting the dog to join him.

Barbara objected. "David, he can't *see*. What are you doing?" But David knew you could also *see* with the heart. At his deepest, most intuitive level, David understood that Skidboot loved only one thing more than David, Barbara and Russell, and that was an *audience*.

I can't deny this dog what is rightfully his. David was adamant, and Barbara bridled, thinking David meant *money*. But no, he meant entertainment, the wonderful boost that occurred to man or dog when people exchanged love.

Love. The entire story.

Calls flooded in, but one call in particular held their attention.

"It's Bill Langworthy from *Pet Star*." David said, incredulous. "He's offering a $25,000 prize, and they want Skidboot to compete." David prepared himself for Barbara's refusal, knew she would say *but he's blind, David, how can he perform?* and decided that before tackling it, they'd take Skidboot around a little, just to see how he did.

First, the diner.

With its jaunty harlequin floor, pale blue walls and lipstick red booths, the diner cheered them up. Plus, Skidboot's photo loomed large on the wall, and their entry stirred up friends and neighbors, who clustered around, murmuring "good dog...we love you, Skidboot....be well, buddy."

David thought he'd try out a command or two. Rising to go wash his hands, he tapped the seat, telling Skidboot to "save my place." New words to Skidboot, and a new concept to carry out in his newly-darkened state. Always game, he jumped up to the vacant seat and "guarded" David's spot. As people applauded, David saw Barbara, teary-eyed, nod at him. Her smile said it all, that she understood. Taking Skidboot back out on the road was not opportunism, not taking advantage, but giving the dog back what he loved, a chance to work.

CHAPTER FIFTY-FIVE

Old Dog, New Tricks

A dog is man's best friend, ask anyone. But if you ask the dog, he might respond with different thoughts, something like:

Goodness. Happy. More happy.

A dog's innocence could shine forth, then be reflected back by the people who see him. Skidboot, nearly iridescent with delight when he entertained, possessed both a lively instinct for mischief as well as for good.

Ask the little blind girl, Topanga, at the Joe Martin Early Childhood Disease Center in Quinlan. Along with the rest of the class, she loved to hear Skidboot and David perform. What she couldn't see, she imagined and giggled at David's humorous patter, his corny jokes, his interaction with his dog. At the end of each routine, Skidboot's reward was to treat himself to a good rummage through the children's toy box—rabbits, stuffed animals, legos, blocks. Somehow, he knew to treat the toys delicately, not to rip and shred them in the usual way. He would sniff and roll them, as if evaluating a fine wine. Then he danced with them, threw them in the air...breathing in the cheerful, soapy, child scent.

Thoughtfully, he would only gum the toys a little, then put them back,

After one performance, Topanga rose to go and hug David, but couldn't find her stick. *Oh, no, she needs her walking device.* David looked up, down and around the room, but no stick.

Skidboot immediately understood. He pranced over to a closet door that had been thrown open, hiding the stick behind. He nosed he door open, carefully picked up her stick, and walked it over to little Topanga.

Skidboot, like all animals, could sense *otherness*, the presence of disability, even disease and his heart moved toward that person.

Often, this happened in reverse. As with Doris Canton.

Doris reached out to Skidboot one day after the Cooper rodeo. It was well into Skidboot's entertainment career, and by now the money was rolling in, the crowds larger than ever. But a crowd is faceless, only an aggregate, with no trace of the individual. This changed as the sixtyish woman, heavyset, waited patiently by the exit as the crowd filtered out. Solid as a pier, her eyes alive with inquiry, she parted the human tide as she waited for the last of the crowd to leave before her words tumbled out.

"What a wonderful dog," she moved toward them. David, always courtly, agreed that he surely was, and instructed Skidboot to say "hello."

As Doris reached down to pat him, her curly black wig slid off her head, revealing the barren landscape of chemotherapy, causing her to blush, apologize and struggle to realign the mop of hair while David tried not to notice, to give her time to collect herself. Skidboot lacked false modesty. He sailed straight over and buried his nose in her now-sitting form. He whimpered, then crooned a little sound that David had never heard before. He stretched up to lick her face, his eyes tender. *Poor woman.*

Doris snuffled, wiped her eyes. She told them how much joy she'd found in Skidboot's performance, how she'd come to see them several times, had seen him on TV and felt a special connection. Love flew back and forth, a love blizzard between Skidboot and Doris as they nuzzled and murmured, and finally, reluctantly, parted ways. Skidboot watched her go, his eyes glued to her retreating form.

David stood amazed and humbled, seeing in the little dog dimensions of sympathy he'd never expected. He reminded himself to call Barbara that night and tell her about Doris, about how loving Skidboot was.

CHAPTER FIFTY-SIX

Seeing Is Believing

Ten shaved heads gleamed like eggs. Not aliens, only youngsters in the Children's Oncology Center in Dallas, who now giggled and laughed at the antics of the blind Skidboot, who fetched toys and listened to the count and let himself be petted until his back shimmied. Even sightless, Skidboot loved to perform. The audience, knowing that the dog could not see, was spellbound. His disability mirrored their own self-doubts, and his continued efforts were an inspiration.

David had altered their routine. One day, he introduced the idea of touch, putting the toy in front of Skidboot, who froze in place as if he could see it. Then David said, "don't get that toy until I touch your paw," and lightly David brushed Skidboot's paw, telling him, "this is your hand. And when I touch your paw, you go get it." At every paw pat, Skidboot would pounce on the toy. From the dog's paw, David moved up to the furry forehead, the side of his foot, but no matter where David touched or patted, Skidboot waited for the light paw-touch. Then, he would pounce.

"Friends," David told the members of the First Congregational Church, the Lion's Club, the Brooke Army Medical Center for the Intrepid, the Handicapped

Rehabilitation Center and the Boles Elementary school in Quinlan, "this dog is 13-years-old, blind, and he is learning new tricks. Now what does that mean for us?"

Huge smiles stretched across the borders of fatigue and discouragement as they grabbed the optimism of Skidboot. Others read about the dog in a lengthy piece in the *Texas County Reporter*, and upon the advent of internet and viral videos, millions more, worldwide, would come to know about the blind dog.

Letters and calls still poured in—(years later it would be emails and text messages by the thousands and web hits by the millions). They eddied and swirled, smothering the Hartwig's doubts.

Oddly enough, it was now Barbara pushing for the *Pet Star* competition. "I thought you wanted to protect him from all that, Barbara?" David couldn't figure her out.

But her motives were clear. She'd seen Skidboot inch his way along to find a toy, seen him waggle his nose at his the cheering crowds, seen the way his coat rippled back and forth, as if he were shivering inside from excitement. How could you keep a dog from doing what he did so well? Would you keep a bird from singing?

"It's about trust, isn't it?" Barbara smiled as she aimed his own words back at him, and David had to admit, she was right. *Pet Star* had now given them a big project to work on, with new training and the heady possibility of winning—and winning big. It would energize them all.

And David realized that they needed Pet Star as much as Skidboot did. *Life is peculiar*, David thought. *And so are we.*

CHAPTER FIFTY-SEVEN

Walking the Pet Star Plank

A carrot.

Everyone needed a carrot to strive after, and *Pet Star* was their carrot.

It dangled out in front of them, getting them up early in the morning to devise and practice new tricks, to work with Skidboot as if he were a rodeo star. It gave them lively conversations at night, as everyone encouraged everyone else. Why, they all thought, a blind dog seemed to heal the family rifts, conjugate their differences.

"Is he eating enough?" Barbara wondered.

"You think we should clean the yard up, maybe move some of that construction stuff?" David was afraid Skidboot might collide with the wheelbarrow, or worse, the cattle in the pen.

"Let's let him talk to Russell," David suggested. Skidboot love Russell, would give a sharp little bark if he heard Russell's name. Now that he was gone, Skidboot moped around his boy's room, sniffing the old boots, the baseball glove, the neatly hung shirts he'd outgrown.

Sometimes, Skidboot would whimper, as if begging to talk to Russell.

"Here boy," David handed him the phone. From the eager tilt of his head, they could tell he heard his name coming over the line, "Skidboot, you okay, boy?" and "Skidboot, you practicing hard?" and so on. Skidboot panted a bit, shaking his head to adjust his spiky ear to the receiver. He nuzzled closer, whining. *It's Russell, my Russell!* He knew the silly words "f-o-n-e" that David had cooked up as a joke. He knew how to retrieve one when David hid it behind a plant, or under the sofa, or near the magazine rack on that nice woman's TV show—Oprah. But he couldn't figure out how *his boy Russell* had become this tiny, tiny voice buried inside.

Skidboot waited patiently until the voice said goodbye, then whined as David took it away.

"Ready to work now?" He could tell that Skidboot was motivated and decided that the usual routine of touching his snout, his back, his tail, his belly then letting him spring forth at the touch on the paw was, well, good, but David had something better in mind. And it involved a touch of risk.

The barrels were about five-yards apart. The plank laid across them was four-feet from the ground. Not exactly a tightrope scene but enough to cause Barbara to clutch Skidboot to her chest, holding him tight in protest.

"A blind dog, walking a plank, what are you thinking of?"

David shuffled a little, then told her that he was thinking of a *blind dog walking a plank*, that's what he was thinking of. He explained that Skidboot, like *everyone*, needed a challenge. He'd mastered the touch-a-paw-retrieve-a-toy routine even though handicapped and was clearly ready for something new. Like this.

David scooped Skidboot up to the top of the barrel, where he teetered, his nose sniffing actively, trying the wind in every direction.

Barbara was not convinced and told David that it was *his* challenge he was working on, using the dog. But David just continued. He spoke to Skidboot calmly, urging him along the beam. *I'm gonna be here with you buddy, you just walk slowly. One foot, another foot, that's the way. Keep your feet moving, buddy, let's go.*

Skidboot held his nose toward the plank, sniffing a path. His paws prized slowly along the scabby wood, nails scrabbling as he memorized its feel, its width and length. Suddenly, one paw slipped off the beam and Skidboot pitched forward, a flurry of frantic legs and beating tail.

"It's ok Skidboot, steady boy." David caught him, cradled him briefly, but Skidboot fought the embrace to get back on the beam.

"Look at that, Barbara. Blind balance!"

Skidboot, back on the beam, nearly pranced with excitement. *The plank! He could feel it!*

Every day thereafter was Plank Day, with Skidboot inching, slipping and prancing along the plank. He had a movement for every inch of the board and loved to hear David announce: "And now, ladies and gentlemen, we have our dog, Skidboot, *walking the plank!*"

Skidboot was now seasoned as a buccaneer, and by the following Tuesday, as the Buffalo grass rustled gently in the spring air and Straggler Daisies poked through the warming soil, a quivering dog, nose high, minced across a 10-foot beam like a fashion model and then back again. And then turned and repeated his path. Again and again.

Barbara, washing dishes in the kitchen, watched. She wiped her eyes and then remembered her soapy gloves. *Even more to cry about now,* she smiled and turned away.

CHAPTER FIFTY-EIGHT

Trembling Towards Success

"Mr. Hartwig, they're ready for you."

He'd been dreading these words. He heard these words in his nightmares, and just a minute ago, had felt sick to his stomach with anxiety. He could never figure out why *he* was so upset while Skidboot, the one who couldn't even see, seemed like a poster child for canine sanguine.

Calm. Bright eyed. Eager to perform.

In fact, the night before, they'd watched *Pet Star*, and David pointed out why Skidboot had more to offer than the dancing pig, the Cocker Spaniel that twirled or — what next, the cat speaking English? When the bulldog on a skateboard whizzed across stage, Skidboot, even without seeing it, let out a rare howl. David laughed, and then he, too, let out a howl. And they ended the *Pet Star* show by diving under a pillow and upsetting the bowl of popcorn, two television critics having their say.

"Skidboot," David laughed, dusting off popcorn, "it doesn't get any better, does it boy?"

What followed the next day was a first class flight, a four-star hotel and their arrival at the Pet Star studios, while still enjoying the last-minute improv trick they'd played at the airport. David noticed how he always said "they" and realized that he, too, was basking in the stardom.

The "trick" had been fun. About to hand over his ticket, David hesitated, then told Skidboot to take it over instead. The slightly bored attendant, accustomed to watching children, the disabled, sports folks, rock stars, baseball teams, giggling girls, and squalling families board the plane, had yet to take a ticket from a dog.

Until then.

He pranced up, snout lifted high, the ticket delicately held at the edge, as if he knew that too much bite would deface it, and offered it to her as she brushed her hair aside, bent down, and laughed, "look! It's a dog with a ticket!" Others glanced over, then murmured. Coffee cups stalled in mid-sip, magazines fluttered, cell phones went unanswered at the sight.

Take it! Skidboot felt a tiny bit impatient, and rattled the ticket at her.

"He wants me to take it!" she squealed, and delighted by the carnival aspect, clapped her hands. Again, the little dog had enchanted people. It happened all the time. David had been proud then. Proud many times, actually.

And now, they were about to go onstage, the man with his blind dog, a different team than when Skidboot's vision was 20-20. David knew that the idea of a blind dog would focus interest on Skidboot's dark eyes, and he decided to blindfold him.

Hold still, Skidboot. They'd practiced this before, and Skidboot patiently let him slip the scarf over his eyes. Only one advantage struck David, at least Skidboot wouldn't be distracted by the bright lights, the dangling speakers, the fly cams and mini-cams and humming, clacking, motorized paraphernalia of the television world.

"Just remember, Skidboot," David whispered to him, "there's only one you. No one will ever be anything like you!"

As if agreeing, Skidboot put his paw on David's knee and patted him. Once. Then twice.

Again, the invitation.

"Mr. Hartwig, they're ready for you."

The first trick was the "is it safe to eat the treat" trick, where Skidboot kept a dog treat stuck in his mouth, refusing to gulp it down until David had completely read the list of ingredients, pondered it a bit, then finally given permission with, "enjoy!" The treat vanished, and Skidboot smiled and sat back on his haunches, ready for another routine.

They decided to go with a "canine chat," an aspect of the Skidboot show that always brought laughs. David asked, "what next?" and Skidboot barked "rr-rrr!" David, understanding the reply, said "barrels? You want to do barrels?" and Skidboot, in sync, yowled back at him, *of course I do!* "But wait," David said, "Isn't that dangerous for an old dog in your shape?" and Skidboot, anxious now, barked, "rrr-RRRR!" and nearly slapped David with his paw. Not the nice, pretty-please "tap tap" usually employed, but a big whap, as in, "let's GO!"

The audience, unprompted, burst out laughing.

David shrugged, as in "you asked for it buddy," and led Skidboot over to the plank-and-barrel contraption the crew had set up. The plank hovered about five feet from the floor, bridging two barrels ten yards apart. Carefully, David hoisted the blindfolded dog onto the starting end and secured his feet solidly in the middle of the plank.

"Careful, little buddy. You can do it, boy." As the drums rolled and people leaned forward in their seats, Skidboot took a shaky step. One, then two, then with more confidence, he inched along toward the middle. Then, the unthinkable. In a flash, he'd misplaced one paw and tumbled straight off the board, landing with a "thud" on the ground. He lay there, a pile of speckled fur, without a sound for minutes. The crowd gasped, voices called out, "Skidboot!"

At the army base, Russell and his pals yelled, "no!" Russell dove for the phone to call Barbara, but then saw David rush over, remove the blindfold and tell Mario, "he's ok. Just give him a minute."

A commercial slid into place, a jingly ad for dog chow.

The crowd, now behaving much like a rodeo crowd, began to chant, "Skidboot! Skidboot!" When the dog struggled up, looked around, and gave a short bark, they applauded. Skidboot whined, pawed David's knee and nosed toward the balance board. Again.

"Okay, Skidboot. If you want to..." David slipped the blindfold over his face, hoisted him up, and as the drums rolled and the silence grew, Skidboot, fleet of foot and sure as an arrow, swiftly trotted across.

The crowd erupted with cheers, whistles, cries.

Mario exclaimed, "amazing! Incredible!" Emotions flooded in like high tide, and minutes later, when Mario Lopez stood in front of the assembled contestants, watched the pig grunt, the Cocker Spaniel pirouette, the rest of the proudly leashed animal life cavort, whine, posture and prance — he had only one thing to say.

"Skidboot! The gold medal goes to Skidboot!"

Again, David felt like he was living some kind of golden myth. They'd been one of the top three finalists, and when the audience voted for their favorite pet, a problem arose.

"David," confided Mario, "Big problem. Everyone voted for Skidboot. Not a single vote for any other animal. And because of that, we had to vote again, just to get a runner-up. "

Like a dream, David thought he'd wake up the next morning *without* the grand prize. And then he realized that was not a dream, that yes, they'd won the money, and yes, it was hard-won, but that also yes, it would be out of his hands—gone, redistributed to his investors before even earning bank interest. He sighed, briefly enjoying the sight of all those zeroes…maybe he'd photocopy it, just to remember.

Their return to Quinlan, like a war veteran's military cortege, fluttered with flags, banners and posters thrummed with the bold music. Balloons shot out of mailboxes and dangled gaily from the oak trees. The town had outdone itself to honor its furry hero, and when Barbara ran down the path to greet them, arms wide open, David felt that the last piece was in place.

All that remained was to cash that check, admire the cascade of big bills that flew across the counter as the teller dealt them out like Vegas, and seal them up in individual envelopes, addressed to each sponsor. It was the right thing to do: pay off a debt, one envelope at a time. He'd be doing a lot of driving that day. A lot of envelope delivery, but it was well worth it.

CHAPTER FIFTY-NINE

One Last Game

Sundown lingers, then sighs away. The remains of the day, like fingers raking down the sky, vanish into the horizon. Light dims, slides away and is gone. The twilight gleams with memories, and life tilts sideways, then empties out. But when? What moment? How much time...? You never know.

Is it during vacation? While they lounged on the beach in Corpus Christi, watching Skidboot nip at the waves?

"Look at him," Barbara whispered. Like a child, he flung himself, chest out, into the waves, then splash! And he submerged. Then splash! He bobbed up again. Then under, unseeing but delighted. Then up, bobbing again. Smiling, they murmured about their dog.

"The fact that he's a dog never interfered with his ambition....!"

"Whatever else is gone, it's sure not his energy.... ...! "

"He gives mixed breed a new name: mixed up!"

They laughed, giggled a little, sipped lemonade, while peace, for the first time in many years, flowed softly around them.

Perhaps the moment would happened later, back in Quinlan, on a strange, moonless night in the mobile home at 3 AM, when Skidboot cut straight into the bedroom, whining and worrying. He tugged David's covers off, nearly rolling him out of bed. "Wha?" David, groggy and dazed, sat up. "What's the matter?" Coyotes? Burglars? Skidboot nudged David's hand out from the covers and began to lick it, whining anxiously. David foggily thought back to the javalina incident....*maybe he knows something, some danger.*

He pushed himself from warm nest, struggled with his boots, thinking maybe it was time for carpet slippers and limped after Skidboot. The dog headed straight into the living room, and nosing carefully around, found the rubber football. He grabbed it, felt his way along the wall toward David and bobbed up and down.

"Football? At 3 AM?" David knew the nuances by now, but this was new. Skidboot perched on hind legs, scratching at the door with his paws, the football clutched in his jaws. He wanted to play!

"Ok, boy. But just for a minute."

The flat grassy area felt in front of the trailer lay dark and foreboding. No light touched its dips and draws, and David had to guide Skidboot through the dark. Skidboot whined to keep him on course, and they finally arrived at "their" tree, the tree where he'd trained Skidboot to paw, to swipe, to communicate. Skidboot eagerly pawed the tree, once, twice, then turned unseeing eyes toward David. His eyebrows arched, questioning.

"Sure, boy." David encouraged.

Skidboot patted David's boot. Once, twice, his paw smacking down hard.

"Hey, there Skidboot. Take it easy!"

Skidboot patted and pawed again, whining.

"Ok, let's play ball!" They frolicked, the ball rolling back and forth, flubbing underfoot as they pranced, jigged and whirled in nighttime revelry—a furious, zany, mindless Satyr icon of man and beast, legs and limbs, barks, whines and laughter.

A light flipped on, and Barbara, shimmery and distant, looked out at them frolicking. *My boys.* She yawned. Tomorrow would bring the answers, and not in a happy way. Tomorrow might bring the *moment.* The one they hoped would never come.

CHAPTER SIXTY

End of an Era

Morning. Bird trill, gentle light. The deep hurry of coffee, gulped at the kitchen table. But as David sat, still sleep dazed, something seemed amiss. Skidboot's bed, empty, told of the dog's nocturnal rambles, possibly sniffing around for mice, maybe a midnight snack. Ever since the blindness, Skidboot's patterns had shifted, and they never really knew what to expect.

"Skidboot?" More of a lazy inquiry, as in *where are you, boy?*

After breakfast, as David strolled toward the barn, the inquiry picked up.

"Skidboot?" Where the heck…?

This was different. *Where was his dog?* He never went anywhere without Skidboot sniffing and bounding by his side, and now with the blindness, he usually stayed closer than ever. David strolled around the perimeter of the property, thinking that Skidboot might have done a little cattle chasing, just for old time's sake. *What next, maybe chickens?* David smiled, thinking back on those hellish days, amazed, all over again, at how far they'd come.

Then something caught his attention.

A stillness, where there should have been motion.

A space, unfilled.

A ruffle of fur, animated only by the breeze.

He saw Skidboot under the "pawing" tree, their tree, and his posture, thrown straight, legs stiff, was as unnatural as his stillness.

"Skidboot!" The cry was pure anguish, speaking loss, mourning, even a last-minute crazy urge to "count" him back to life. Maybe if he heard "one-two-THREE...?"

David strode over to the limp form, kneeled beside him, his head bent in mourning. Then, with a sigh, he acknowledged the end of the dream, a friendship, a miracle, a frenzy of daily delight—the end of an era. He scooped Skidboot up in his arms and walked into the future, a place of bleakness, at least for a while.

EPILOGUE

Skidboot, gone.

But never, never forgotten.

In fact, in passing, he grew in memory, taking on a virtual life that brought Barbara and David to the Fess Parker Doubletree Resort in Santa Barbara, California one sultry beachfront evening, a little more than a few months later. Dressed to the hilt, they stood in tuxedo and spangles, Barbara glamorous and David handsome, surveying the waving palms and the blue beach horizon. The sign, "pet friendly" nearly brought tears. Instead, they giggled.

He would have loved those waves. He would have sucked down one of those ginger mint lemonades. He would have camped out on the balcony and watched the stars.

And, he would have been proud of them both, gowned and groomed and outfitted like movie stars, part of an elegant crowd gathered in the grand ballroom at a black tie pet rescue gala. Not just part, but the star couple!

As so many times before, David anticipated his name sounding over the microphone. Calling him to the calf roping contest. Calling him out to perform with Skidboot. And now, calling him up to speak, off the cuff, to hundreds of upscale dog lovers, people who had known Skidboot and wanted to hear a memorial talk. His stomach clutched in the same old way, but incredibly, he took a long, clean breath, straightened up and strode up to the stage.

He told them what they already knew but just wanted to hear again.

That Skidboot was more than his actions, his counting, fetching, dropping dead, fake limping. He was more than his breed, Blue Heeler, descended back to a dingo. He was more than the money he unleashed into the Hartwig's life, as pleasant a surprise as it had been. He was the sum of his parts and more, a direct infusion of love to his friends, his family, his audience. The supercharged little dog could shoot love like an arrow, and it pierced every heart; no one went away from a Skidboot show grumpy, glum or self-involved. With a flip and a smile, Skidboot conveyed love, and, well folks, David continued. *It's our job to keep up the good work.*

Applause rang out, shaking the crystal chandeliers, shimmering the wall-length ballroom mirrors. Even in his passing, Skidboot could still rock an audience, especially with the showing of a special Skidboot video which looped together children's stories about Skidboot, Barbara's first encounter with him, the Letterman, Leno and Oprah shows, his injury.

More cheering. A standing ovation. David thought he felt a gentle tap on his knee, and looked down, expecting to see his dog. But no, he'd brushed the table leg. All he had now was the memory of Skidboot.

Until the next week.

The doorbell rang. David rustled down his newspaper, noting that bad news weighed so heavy that the paper collapsed on its own. *Bad news, all the time.*

Barefoot, he limped over to the door and threw it open. He saw the basket covered with a blanket and his first thought was, *abandoned baby?* That's all he and Barbara needed right now, with Russell starting his law practice. A baby.

The bundle whimpered, *Of course not, don't be a fool!*

The Blue Heeler puppy stared up at him, eyes still milky, nose wet, its pink tongue darting about. He clutched a squeaky toy in his mouth, and as David bent down to pick him up, he bit down hard with a fierce little growl.

"Ok, boy! Take it easy now." David grinned, looking at the mini-Skidboot. The puppy was sired by Skidboot's nephew and would launch many lively, squirming Skidboot progeny, so to speak. Specifically, they were part ABCA Registered Border Collie, one of five boys and four girls, all with color, collars and masks.

"Barbara!" David called back into the house. "Close your eyes. I've got a surprise for you."

AUTHOR'S BIO

Photo by Andrea Young

Cathy Luchetti has written seven books on American history; three have won prestigious national awards: *Women of the West,* the Pacific Northwest Booksellers Award; *Medicine Women,* runner-up for the Willa Cather Award; *Home on the Range,* the James Beard Award, and *The Hot Flash Cookbook,* an international cookbook prize. After college, Cathy joined the Peace Corps and lived for two years in remote villages in Colombia, South America. She has spoken frequently on NPR and been featured in several television documentaries.

Cathy enjoys backpacking, mountain scrambling and desert exploration. Her current books-in-progress focus on adventure, risk, and uncertainty. She lives in the Northern California with her husband Peter. Cathy's humorous and informative talks have been popular around the country, including the National Archives, the Library of Congress, the Nevada Humanities Council, the Junto Society and more.

BACKSTORY

It was September, 2007, a year and a half since my exit from the military. I sat at my desk sifting through emails and noticed one with the subject: 'The Amazing Skidboot.' It was a forwarded email that I nearly deleted, but decided not to when considering that the sender, my father-in-law, would later quiz me on it. I clicked on the Youtube link. The first couple of minutes revealed to me nothing distinguishing this dog from any other who performed basic tricks like 'fetch,' but then something happened that caused me to scroll back and watch several times over. Skidboot's owner, David Hartwig commanded his dog: "wave your left hand, wave your right hand, wave your left hand, now turn around, turn the other way, ease up on it, now touch it," and without fail, Skidboot complied. It was then that I was convinced that this dog was, in fact, 'amazing.' By the end I was choked up and filled with inspiration. Growing up with favorite movies like *Old Yeller* and *Where the Red Fern Grows*, I said to myself, *that's a movie!* and was sold on watching it in the theaters whenever it came out.

I then searched the internet for a release date expecting to see a Disney trailer but was surprised to find nothing. After forwarding the email to my friends, I went on with my life.

Two years later I received a newsletter with another link to the Skidboot story and watched again repeating the same sentiments. I again searched the internet for a movie trailer or Hollywood press release reporting the film's release date. I was baffled after finding zilch. *How was this possible?*

In early 2011, I received yet another email with a link for Skidboot, searched the internet, same result. It was then that I decided to find out why a story so big would fizzle to so little. Evidently, no movie studio had picked it up. I called my good friend and fellow screenwriter, Guillermo Machado, and asked him if he would be willing to partner with me on the development of the Skidboot project. He expressed interest peppered with apprehension. Tongue-in-cheek, he said — suspecting my chances at slim to none — that if I could secure the story rights, he might commit.

I immediately searched for David Hartwig's number, and quickly realized he resided just outside of Dallas, Texas. I called and reached a voice-mail with David's voice: "thanks for the call, leave a message." Within hours, he returned my call. I expressed my love for their story and how it begged for a theatrical release, then described how Guillermo and I authored a screenplay in 2000 that gained a lot of attention and how I had a deep desire to take a crack at drafting a movie script for Skidboot.

"Well, come on up then," David replied.

The following weekend, I drove my two girls to the Hartwig ranch in Quinlan. We toured the grounds and Skidboot's burial site, beneath an old oak tree. We rode horses, fed calves and played with Skidboot's offspring. By the end of the day, David and I shook hands, deciding to move forward with the development of the Skidboot project. Soon after, we wrote the script.

Fast forward two years, and here we are today. It has been a long road, littered with Starbucks coffees, conference calls, dinners, meetings, *meetings* about meetings along with all sorts of diverse obstacles. Over and again we were told "great story, but not commercial enough," and that has translated into the one constant that followed David and Skidboot throughout their lives: underdogs, without a shot in the dark, and yet, theirs has always been a story that resonated well with people, pet lovers or not, children and adults. Because of this, we felt it deserved to be shared with the rest of the world. And with that driving force, I would reach out to renowned Texas author, Cathy Luchetti, and within no time, she would express the same enthusiasm to join the Skidboot team. It has been our deepest privilege and honor to work with both her and David ... only wish I could've met Skidboot.

—Joel Carpenter, Project Skidboot

The Skidboot legacy continues in NY Times Square

Made in the USA
Lexington, KY
29 December 2013